170
043r

118510

DATE DUE			

Reflections
on
Life and Death

The Aesthetics of Modernism
Anthology of French Poetry
Art and Knowledge
Britain and France, the Unruly Twins
Columbus's Isle
Contemporary French Poetry
Corsica, the Scented Isle
The Eagle of Prometheus (*poems*)
T. S. Eliot, Poet and Dramatist
France and the War
France and the Problems of Peace
The French Contemporary Theatre
Impressions of People and Literature
Landmarks of Contemporary Drama
Lights in the Distance (*poems*)
Mary Stuart (*verse play*)
The Necessity of Being
Paradoxes (*poems*)
The Poetic Drama of Paul Claudel
Realism and Imagination
Reflections on the Theatre (*translation*)
Religion and Modern Society
Symbolism—from Poe to Mallarmé
The Time of the Rising Sea (*poems*)
Twentieth-Century French Thought
White Temple by the Sea (*poems*)

Reflections
on
Life and Death

JOSEPH CHIARI
Docteur ès Lettres

GORDIAN PRESS
NEW YORK
1977

Copyright © 1977 by Joseph Chiari

Published by Gordian Press, Inc.
85 Tompkins Street
Staten Island, New York 10304

Printed in Great Britain

Library of Congress Cataloging in Publication Data
Chiari, Joseph.
    Reflections on life and death.

    1. Ethics.   2.   Civilization, Modern.   I.   Title.
BJ1012.C49   170   77–4054
ISBN 0–87752–212–X

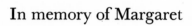

In memory of Margaret

Contents

My spirit has pass'd in compassion and determination
    around the whole earth,
I have looked for equals and lovers and found them
    ready for me in all lands,
I think some divine rapport has equalised me with them.

Walt Whitman: Leaves of Grass

Preface

This book is in praise of life, and a tribute to man—a puny animal clinging to a moss-covered rock caught in the dance of stars and galaxies which form the universe, and outshining all by his patience and courage to live life in the light of impending death, thus testifying to the fact that there is no consciousness without suffering, and no fate that acceptance cannot transcend.

Yet, just as there is no sun without shadows, in the same way some of man's great virtues are much stained by his inhumanity to man. Though life is but a gasp between birth and death, he nevertheless finds it possible to waste part of it in attempts to stifle it in others. Caught, as he is at this moment, between two worlds—one half-dead or swamped in nihilism, and the other struggling to be born—he has partly lost the sense of the Divine, and he is losing now the sense of the human, to the extent that humanism—whether religious or atheistic—has become a tainted word. The sap and honey of life, the throbbings of the heart, the excitements of the mind entranced by the joys of the earth are withered away and replaced by pseudo-scientific abstractions in which there is only room for things, signs, systems, structures, that is to say Frankensteins that have taken over and confined their Maker to limbo. Life is thus reduced to an algebraic formula in which existence is merely a question of a plus or a minus.

Like a tin on a shelf in a supermarket, man is given a label which wipes out his face and thus makes it possible to kill any so-called fascist, communist, colonialist, black or white without any qualms, for the label justifies the act. Yet if man looked beyond it, into the depths of the other man's eyes, he would not fail to discover in every case the same longing for peace, happiness and love, and he would never be able to destroy other men for the sake of political labels or the millennium to come. He would realise, in the light of his awakened consciousness, that every man is living his death, and dying his life, that all men must love one another, for they all die, as Christ died on the Cross, and that only love can redeem death.

After the most savage and destructive wars in history, after Hiroshima, living as he does now under the threat of unparalleled holocausts whose genetic effects could ripple on throughout time's length and possibly turn mankind into something beyond the human imagination, man must realise that the world cannot be ruled by violence or force but, on the contrary, as Nietzsche put it, it can be ruled 'only by thoughts that come on doves' feet'. The Dove is Christ, Buddha, or any avatar of the Divine who adopts its white wings as a symbol of love and peace. But these wings must not be made to shelter any dogmatism, intolerance or attempts to teach or to coerce dissenters, by their rulers or party leaders, through imprisonment, concentration camps or psychiatric treatment. Men must always be given the freedom to fulfil their own rationality and individuality in the family, society or the state, in conditions that respect freedom of conscience and can be universalised, and not in terms of party dogma or nationalistic self-interest which always ignore the true interests of mankind. Uniformity and totalitarianism in all its disguises are, like a tidal wave, creeping over the world from the East, the land of great human masses and autocratic materialism. Faced with this prospect, men must remember that it is never wise to put temptation in the way of anyone who might not be able to resist it. Not every man or state could be expected to show the resilience and, above all, the spirituality of Job, and that is why Nietzsche's words, spoken practically a hundred years ago, should still go on ringing in our minds: 'The disease of the will is suffused unequally over Europe. It is worst and most varied where civilisation has longest prevailed . . . It is therefore in the France of today, as can be readily disclosed and comprehended, that the will is most infirm . . . It is considerably stronger in England, Spain and Corsica, associated with phlegm in the former, and with hard skulls in the latter . . . but it is strongest and most surprising of all in that immense middle empire where Europe, as it were, flows back to Asia—namely Russia. There the power to will has been long stored up and accumulated, where the will—uncertain whether to be negative or affirmative—waits threateningly to be discharged (to borrow their pet phrase from our physicists).' (*Beyond Good and Evil*, Allen & Unwin, 1967, p. 145)

Prudence in avoiding putting temptation in the way of those who might not resist it must not be equated with hostility or indifference. It must, on the contrary, be part of the wisdom which ought to impel us to look upon all men as capable of doing good and loving one another. Love must transcend all the differences that separate men and, in the name of sectional or nationalistic ideologies, enable them to kill with a good conscience. This could not happen if man admitted, or were aware of, a universal moral conscience as the fountain-head of life and morality. Beyond the various churches which at times disunite, and religious creeds which divide men and even encourage them to kill in the name of their truth, there is a supreme truth, which is that all men are brothers in life and in death, that no man, whatever reasons he may give, has the right to destroy what he cannot create, and that each man must be allowed to climb his own Calvary and to stretch himself on his cross, in the arms of Death or, if he believes, in the arms of God, in the nakedness of his own conscience, face to face with eternal light and knowledge.

Introduction

Much singed by the slow-burning greenwood of life, still haunted by questions unanswered, I should like, while I may, to make some comments about certain problems which confront mankind at this moment. From the top of the hill where I now find myself, with the sun westering low on the horizon, looking back at the ground covered, and at the land ahead—a land too broad for me to explore—a sense of fellow-feeling for all those engaged in life's journey compels me to offer encouragement about some directions, and caution about others. My experience is that of a man who has suddenly passed from rural life, ruled by the light of the sun and the rise and fall of the seasons, to a world of trains, planes, journeys to the moon and rockets to Mars and Venus, and from solitary walks along paths often crossed by sly, indifferent foxes or harrassed, anxious boars rushing through the brushwood, to the crowded pavements of Sauchihall Street, Princes Street or Piccadilly Circus. The sun surging like a giant chalice from the sea, the moon trailing silver over it, the passing shadows of ships on the horizon, the tinkling of goats' bells on the hillside, the dance of bees around the oak tree where they nested, the processions of ants, the antics of lizards on rocks, hawks swooping on scared pigeons, and snakes pushing down their sausage-like throats unwilling frogs and toads, were my daily films. The poppies in the fields nodded assent or dissent, nettles and thorns taught me the don'ts of Nature, and wild strawberries hidden under bracken in chestnut woods were more exciting than any gold rush. Trains were mythological animals competing with bulls and cows unwilling to yield to them the overlordship of the plains.

15

Born into a world which was that of ancient Greece, where the weekly bread was still baked in the communal oven, and the weekly washing was done by the Nausicaas of the village in mountain streams, with nearby bushes beflagged with drying clothes, I moved from this world where time was told by the shadow of the oak tree and the hooting of the owl, to a world in which the notion of communal oven has ceased to mean bread and life, and only brings to mind Dachau and Auschwitz, and where the word 'trench' no longer means potatoes and well-blanched celery, but Katyn and other mass-graves in which man's savagery has buried his soul. I moved from the days when an El Greco-like Christ nailed upon a cross wound its way through the village in the glare of torchlights on Good Friday, to the empty churches of big metropolises and the sham claims of new Christs.

These claims are vain, for whether Christ was the son of God or the greatest incarnation of genius the world has ever known, the result is the same. He sums up in his vision the wisdom of Socrates and Plato, the passionate love of man of the Jewish prophets, and a capacity to lift man out of the earth which rejoins and transforms the dream of Buddha, for he cares not only for the soul, but also for man's battered body, source of pains and joys, yet desperately needed, both in order to know himself and to be known as himself, by his Creator. Twenty centuries lived in his light, at times distorted, often misused, and even turned into apocalyptic darkness, have taken man from the shores of Attica and Judaea to the shores of the moon and knowledge of the stars, and this he has done not in spite of Christ, as some detractors of religion carelessly assert, but because of him, for it was the Christian Church and Christian teaching that revived the Greek love of science, mathematics and rationalism, and created and maintained, for a long time, most of the schools of Western Europe. The foundations of modern rationalism and the scientific attitude were laid by churchmen. Roger Bacon, Abelard, William of Ockham and other monks inaugurated the pragmatism and experimentalism that were later to be developed by Locke, Newton and other scientific minds. Luther, Erasmus and Giordano Bruno, to quote only a handful of very unconventional men, were trained in monasteries like most Renaissance philosophers.

Now that science and scientific discoveries have transformed the world more deeply in fifty years than in twenty centuries, now that the rhythm of life has passed from the progressive pattern of growth in all domains to a succession of jumps and upheavals which transform the mind as well as the body, together with the means to cope with them, man unavoidably stands perplexed and wondering what hand, what guiding light will help him to find the way ahead, and prevent him from being swept away by his passions, his instincts, and by the power conferred upon him by his demiurgic discoveries. He feels that he is by himself, and no longer himself; he has been repeatedly told that God is dead, that he himself is probably so too, and that he is about to be replaced by computers, by all sorts of abstract forces which act on their own and which will henceforth float him on their billows like the flotsam and jetsam of long-lost civilisations. What can he do? Which way should he turn?

Science, which is inherent in man, but is not the whole man, has transformed the life of the planet, which now, thanks to it, lives, and will die, as one organic unit. Knowledge of life as it is now is world-wide; the poor of Africa and India know all about the rich life of the highly industrialised Western nations, including Russia, which hobnobs with the poor, subverts and patronises them, and gives them guns instead of bread, but itself lives the life of the rich, and is more terrifyingly rich and powerful than all nations except one. The poor nations are no longer prepared to live down their poverty as a curse of fate, original sin or anything else; they want their share of the good life of the earth, and either they will have it or the earth will burst because of it. The whole world lives by the same single clock, listens to the same news, covets the same cars, the same refrigerators, hears the same non-musical tunes, dreams of the same pin-ups, and follows with indifference the slaughter of Vietnamese, Angolans or Lebanese. It is all a vast game, a continuous 'happening', kept going for the benefit of television and cinema, in a climate of entertainers and entertained. Whether they like it or not, men are overwhelmingly made aware of the fact that although they share the same fate, the same needs, appetites and dreams, they are not treated as brothers, but as pawns in games between political parties intent on power, between governments and between ideologies, each claiming to know the secret of the good and happy life, and wanting to force it upon everybody else. The two main contending ideologies, of course, are capitalism and Communism, and the alternatives offered are the daemonic oppression of the poor by the rich under the former, and the political oppression of all under the latter.

We live in a world in which scientific knowledge is increasing from day to day, and no man can any longer claim to be able to embrace the whole of it. The age of the admirable Crichton or of Pico della Mirandola is over and will never return. The human brain has remained and will remain the same, for time beyond the present range of thought, but its capacity develops and its scope and content of knowledge increases and will go on increasing. Scientific knowledge is universal, and whatever is now, will be as long as man. We cannot replace the plane by the horse, but the horse will have its place on race courses or on country rides, and who knows what could happen once the petrol reserves are exhausted? Man's great discoveries, the pride of his genius, can neither be abolished nor denigrated. Though scientists discovered the means of splitting the atom, it was the politicians, therefore the man in the street, that is to say every one of us, who decided about the application of the discovery at Hiroshima and Nagasaki. Scientists discover and propose, the politico-social system disposes, and it is the moral code of the latter, or lack of it, that we must hold responsible, not the scientists'. They should only be blamed if and when ambition seals their consciences, and if they do not make their opinions about the use of their discoveries clearly known, and of course, worse still, if they take part in the making of devices or products like poison or bacterial gas, napalm and similar things, which can only be used for destruction and for nothing else. The scientist must neither be the scapegoat of our loveless world nor the new god worshipped amongst the rubble of fallen altars, which his rationality is supposed to have cast down. He has cast down nothing, for religion is neither made nor destroyed by reason. Science is, indeed, an integral part of Western civilisation, for, as Einstein put it, 'science without religion is lame, religion without science is blind.' (A. Mosz-

18

kowski, *Conversations with Einstein*, Horizon Press, New York, 1970, p. 46)

Religion is made not by reason, but by the heart, by the need and longing for it, because it answers man's urge to transcend himself through spirit, and it is destroyed by the heart, when it disappoints man's spirit through compromise, materialism or pure abstraction, which dissociate body from mind and soul, and history from life, for life is all these things and more, since it is part of the perenniality which subsumes them all. Pure spiritualism is just as alien to man as the dogmatic materialism of Marxism; the one ignores biology and economics, the other ignores the heart, the mind, the aspirations of man which are not bound by biology or matter, for matter itself can be defined only in terms of its finality and not of its reality, which is energy, as elusive as the force that holds cells together or propels the sap through flowers and trees. Nothing in life is reducible to simple generalisations, and it is important ever to keep present in the mind Hamlet's words to Horatio:

> There are more things in heaven and earth, Horatio,
> Than are dreamt of in your philosophy.

Life is mysterious, describable perhaps, but indefinable, for one can know only parts of it, but not the whole, and life is a whole of which we ourselves are parts, therefore both knowers and known are parts of the whole. No dogma, scientific or religious, will provide us with the right answers to cope with it and to contribute to its rational, beneficent unfolding in the centuries and millenaries to come. Science is neither philosophy nor religion nor ethics. Philosophy, on the other hand, has something to say about science, religion and ethics, which are all part of it.

There is no rivalry between scientific and metaphysical knowledge. Kant proved it. Each has its respective domain, and if science leads to pragmatic, experimental, verifiable or refutable truths, metaphysics leads to logical truths based on axioms or principles which are not analytical but synthetic and which, therefore, can only be accepted or rejected according to the inclination of the heart and mind which cannot ration-

19

alise them. Religious knowledge, for those who believe in religion, is vital to ethics; on the other hand, experimental knowledge is not. Knowledge of the second law of thermo-dynamics or the behaviour of electrons offers no help in deciding whether I should love my neighbour or advocate the abolition of the death penalty. Therefore, as Apelles quietly whispered to the passing busybody who presumed to criticise his work, 'ne sutor ultra crepidam'—in other words, everyone should mind his onions. Science is a vital human discipline, but it is neither the panacea to cure all ills, nor, of course, the source of man's failings. The notion that science and techno-logical knowledge have outstripped our moral knowledge and sensibility, so that we can no longer rationally cope with life, is both a cliché and an over-simplification of the problems confronting modern man. But if by toying with this notion we mean to suggest that because of the amplitude of our scientific discoveries, we suddenly have the feeling of belonging to a world that no longer conforms with the range of our mental apprehension and moral judgments, or if we feel that we are adrift on an uncharted ocean on a small canoe and no longer safely installed on a well-equipped, well-manned liner, we are certainly right. There has been, because of very swift changes in populations, social structures, range of knowledge, human needs and aspirations, a collapse of religious and moral values, due to the fact that these values have failed to adjust to the changing world. Therefore, this adjustment must urgently be made now; man must now try to reach an equilibrium between frightened, anguished, purposeless individuality and the wide, integrated world to which he belongs. In order to do this, he must stop clinging to ancient prejudices and divinities, and seek, side by side with his fellow-beings, to discover new values or, better still, to rediscover the valuable old ones and the truth he has for so long ignored.

This truth is unifying, reuniting, not divisive. Christ is not against Buddha, Mohammed or Krishna; he is with them, in them, as part of the light man feels in his soul, and with which he seeks to guide his journey on earth. Our Christian duty is not to put out all other neighbouring lights, and insist that ours is the only good and valid one, but to welcome any true light (one cannot, of course, call atheistic Marxism a light, but rather a darkness), any true love, and to walk side by side towards our waiting end. Those who cannot discover a true light by themselves should have the humility to follow those who have better sight, provided that those who ask to be followed are humble enough to be aware of their failings and submit everything they do to the criterion of absolute respect of the other's conscience. Our equalitarian age is averse to any notion of guidance, discipline, respect of other people's freedom, or recognition of one's own mental or affective limitations. Yet one cannot go very far with such prejudices and attitudes. We are certainly all equal as human beings; we are indeed all God's children, and for Him, the beggar is as important as the saint or the genius. But we are not all equals in minds, hearts, imaginations, physical abilities and muscular power.

The world is not entirely made up of Einsteins, Picassos or Bartoks; we cannot all understand the relativity theory, or the *Critique of Pure Reason*; we cannot all be saints, sufis, avatars, Bodhisattvas, revealers of religion, ethical teachers or creative geniuses. But we ought to be prepared to believe that such manifestations of genius or of the Divine exist, and that we could listen to them, use our reason and heart, and take whatever we can or whatever we need, from their wisdom. Each man has something special to contribute, if only he can discover what it is, yet he never will if, instead of looking into himself and assessing his positive as well as his negative aspects, he thinks he is somebody else, or spends his time dreaming of being somebody else. We must get out of our hamlets and villages, and live in open towns which are practically as wide as the world. We must cultivate our sense of truth and beauty, in the certainty that other men too possess one and want to share it with us, and we must remember that we deserve the title of man only if we help the other to get out of himself what is best in him and to share it with others, so as to make a world in which men truly love one another, or at least constantly try to, because there is no other way to live without either killing or being killed.

Reflections

on

Life and Death

I

Time and Eternity

Religions and philosophies have continuously evolved through-out the six thousand years or so that constitute the span of history and civilisation as we know it, and they have constantly interpenetrated and cross-fertilised each other, even at times been coincidental, as is the case with Greek thought and religion, and with Buddhism. Greek religion is above all Greek philosophy from Pythagoras to Plato, and Hindu thought is essentially Buddha's thought. The great religions of the world are like a network of rivers. They all started from the same source—the need for the Divine or for transcendence, and they have spread over the plains, continuously capturing streams from one another, sometimes merging into one, as was the case with the Greek and the Judaic, yet with every one of them retaining accretions that have come to them in the course of their long progress through historical time. Platonism, the main fount of Western mysticism, derived a great deal of its thought from the Orphic and Eleusinian mysteries, from Pythagoras and from Hindu thought which, in itself, had already benefited from Greek thought through the long established contacts that existed between Greece, the Middle East and India.

Religion means to connect, to bind together, and the problem of religion is to link the human with the transcendental, time with eternity. In all religions the Divine or transcendental is perfect, and the human, which is imperfect, must find means, through life, to qualify or make itself fit for union with it. The people of Israel insisted above all on obedience to God's laws; on the other hand, the suffering God of Egypt could only welcome the human creature to His bosom once he had gone

25

through much suffering and death. For Platonism, Christianity, Buddhism or Islam, it is only through nakedness and death that the human being can reach the Divine or Nirvana; it is therefore only out of time, in eternity, that absolute bliss can be achieved.

The body is generally looked upon as the tomb of the soul, a burden from which the soul must rid itself in order to reach perfect knowledge and bliss. Platonism as well as Buddhism stresses the dangers of the flesh, source of endless desires, servitudes, suffering and, therefore, separation from Nirvana, or from the perfect control of oneself advocated by Senecan stoicism which, like Platonism, played an important part in the making of Christianity. To anthropomorphic Protagoras who proudly declared that 'man is the measure of all things', pre-Christian Plato replied: 'God is the true measure of all things.' (*Republic*, VI 504c and *The Laws*, IV 716c). The love of God is for Plato the foundation of the relation between man and the Divine, and the only source of certainty and knowledge. Whatever finality and fulfilment things may achieve in the world takes place according to divine predestination. This is Plato speaking, though it very much sounds like St Augustine, who adapted Platonism to Christianity. The need to shed all attachments to the world, and to go through the night of suffering and unknowing before one can be illumined by the love and truth of God, is essentially Platonic. The passage from the ignorance and darkness of the cave to the true light of God is always painful, and is the paradigm of all great conversions, of nights spent in deserts before illumination comes. St John of the Cross, St Teresa and Christ himself went through this, and the truth that they all finally discovered was the 'truth which the soul apprehended when it was with God, and when it saw the true reality'. (*Phaedrus*, 249 bc)

Every soul, in the Platonic world, comes from God and returns to Him; knowledge is, in fact, reminiscence or memory of the great Memory, and the past is therefore the best image of the eternal reality, to which, in essence, every soul has had access, though only very few retain enough memory of it, or the capacity, to reconnect with it. This is Orphic knowledge, not different from the Augustinian notion of knowledge through God, and the preparation for both is the same—detachment

26

from the world and devoted contemplation, so as to reach the state of receptivity in which Grace or the Divine can bring to us the awareness of truth, or of beauty, which is the same thing, for at such a level beauty and truth are one. The spirit bloweth where it listeth; it does not come at random, it can only come to those who can prepare for it and, in fact, are made for it. It is the same with creative inspiration. One has necessarily to be born an artist to be visited with inspiration, for not everyone can connect with the 'great Memory' and thus know what beauty is. Beauty is a kind of grace, an intuition from another world, from eternity no doubt, and it causes in him who receives it an illumination that impels him to give it shape and to express through it the truth he has lived. The illumination of the saint is not of a different nature; the energy he receives from his illumination, from then on, fills his life and impels him to spread the love that has been imparted to him and to attempt to create a society in which men may be made fit to participate in such a love and such joys, for, as Plato said: 'He who is able, after having reached truth, to bring forth and to foster in himself true virtue, will become God's friend and be immortal, in so far as this is conceded to man.' (*Symposium*, 212 a)

These glimpses or incommunicable visions of the eternal, or of God, are rare, and they can be achieved only through total love which abolishes the self and connects time with eternity. These two concepts, which are the foundation of Heraclitean and Platonic philosophy and of Greek religion, are basic to all religions, and from Heraclitus to our time they have undergone constant fluctuations in meaning; they will probably continue to do so until the end of time. To rehearse their various meanings would take volumes; to claim originality of definition would be presumptuous. Yet my understanding of them is the basis of my approach to religion, nothing more, nothing less, and so should be made clear at the outset.

Time and eternity are not separate entities; they form a kind of continuum out of which man—an existential subject— draws the various concepts of time, space and eternity. The concept of time and that of space are complementary and can be fused into one, for time necessarily implies extension in space, and all in all space can only be conceived of as extended time apprehended by a living subject. Space, in fact, cannot be thought of without time, or outside time. The same applies to the concept of eternity, which can only be thought of from time, and in relation with time. Eternity is primarily what is not time, or what is timeless, and timelessness could not be conceived of without time. Therefore, time is as necessary to eternity as eternity is to time. The two notions cannot be thought of as separate, or sequential; they can only be thought of as one single continuum or intelligible concept, embodying aspects of both; they are so closely intertwined as to be inextricable, so much so that God—the Eternal—can no more be thought of without creation or time than creation can be thought of without God. The two notions are synchronic, as is everything connected with God, therefore creation, as part of eternity, has no more a beginning or an end than God or eternity has a beginning or an end. They are, and they will always be, whatever form time takes or ceases to take, for it is possible to think of a final stage in the dialectical interplay of time with eternity, a stage which will be reached when eternity and time are totally and perfectly united into one single intelligible transcendental reality expressed by one single verb which is the verb 'to be' used in the present indicative.

The present, the eternal, unchanging present contains all possible positive predicates such as goodness, beauty or truth, summed up in one concept—that of eternal self-knowledge. Such a stage cannot be reached as long as time and eternity are separate concepts in the same continuum. That means that as long as the concept of time remains valid, and it will remain so as long as there is subjective existence in the universe, the concept of eternity can be looked upon neither as closed nor as perfectly self-knowing. This stage could only be reached at the end of time, if and when all the possibilities of existence have been exhausted, and that cannot be anticipated, for the renewal of possibilities through existence looked upon from the finite could be considered as infinite, therefore neither time nor eternity would ever end. All the possibilities of time are, of course, present in eternity and known as such in their essential forms, which, because of their positive as well as negative virtualities, can reveal themselves, and therefore be fully known, only through the interactions and positivity of existence.

28

Existence is the outcome of the interplay of positive and negative elements which, from the point of view of eternity, are infinite, for they comprise all the virtualities which might be, or might not be, and which will manifest their positiveness, and therefore their final perenniality, only through existence. Time is thus the midwife of eternity, for only what has been sieved and transmuted by time into real existence can form part of the continuum of eternity. Real existence means here absolute perfection of *ens* or form, that is to say total fulfilment of all the possibilities of essence so as to reach a perfect equilibrium between spirit and matter, and between contending thoughts and feelings, so that the whole is in perfect harmony and therefore conforms with the truth of its essence. This perfection of essence through existence can pertain neither to nature nor to the animal world; it can pertain only to a thinking subject, aware of his finality and of his separation from its source, and therefore longing for union with it and for the perfection of spirit.

God is infinite, positive, open, and ever making His own perfection through creation, which sifts the eternally positive essence from nothingness inherent in creation. God is absolutely perfect as essence, but not perfect in the sense of being closed. Such a state cannot be envisaged, for the virtualities of essence as energy or will-to-being are infinite, and the concept of the infinite is unthinkable as such from the finite. Concepts necessarily belong to the finite, and the basic concept of the finite is itself an *a priori* which is only partly analytical and which necessarily involves the synthetic, intelligible notion of infinite. God is such a notion, which is also the Idea of Plato, something that can be valid only if it predicates infinity or eternity of power and self-creativity. Creation is the tumult of clouds in Michelangelo's Sistine Chapel, in which God's finger injects His creative lightning which makes life. It is a turbulence of forms, ceaselessly flowing and changing, uniting and breaking apart, ever combining with more and more complex entities, which dissolve again and again into elementary forms, until they have fulfilled themselves, that is to say until they have reached the eternal, through existence. Creation is the will to being, through the becoming of time, enfolding into its eternal sameness life and death, light and darkness, construction and destruction, as unavoidable as the cycles of the seasons. It is God's dream, illuminating with His light the multitudinous leaves of the tree of life, gilding its thoughts and hopes, and consuming the dead branches and foliage into the nothingness which His incandescence eternally negates.

God cannot be absolutely self-knowing, as long as there is time, through which He actualises the absolute self-knowledge which He is in eternity. God cannot be conceived of as stillness, or a closed perfection, for true perfection is not fixity but tension towards total harmony which must be always receding, for, if reached, it would mean infinite motionlessness, absolute lack of essence-for-being, that is to say non-being, and God cannot be conceived of as non-being. Christ, begotten from God, therefore God as essence or logos of creation, is God's temporal separation from Himself, not in order to redeem man, since man as man can never have been lost for God, but in order to testify to Himself through His creation that His truth is love, and nothing else. Christ's coming to earth testifies to the truth that creation is God-made, since its beginning, and God-informed, until the enfolding of time into eternity, and that God loves creation and Christ as Himself, because they are Himself, so that God is nothing else but love, which is, in the end, the only incontrovertible ontological truth.

Every man, informed with God's spirit, makes himself and God through time, and at the end of his time, that is to say at death, he has made himself what he truly is and what he will be in eternity. There is, thus, no need of weighing, or of examining and testing his past life. What he truly is is what he appears to be. Good and evil have woven their patterns through his life, and at death his soul or essence, which has been ground by the continuous life-conflict between good and evil, has reached the stage of what it will truly be in eternity. At death the human being does not confront eternity as an empty vessel or a shell into which eternity pours the substance and the eternal reality which will make of him what he will be for ever; he himself has secreted this eternal substance and eternal reality through his actions, feelings and thoughts. Throughout his conscious and subconscious life, he has sieved the good from the bad, the true from the false, the positive from the negative, by constantly seeking or failing to realise the truth of his essence, which is his true relationship and bond with God; and he will be more or less near to God according to the degree of essence or love he had in himself, and according to the extent to which he actualised this essence in time. The saint, for instance, has a constant awareness of his essence, of his integration in nature, and of his total dependence upon God; therefore, he has with God the constant closeness that his essence requires; he is at the very heart of light, the still centre of the living universe, which, since this cannot be made perfectly coincidental with creation in time, makes it necessary for the good and evil of time to have their correspondence in eternity.

As long as creation is subject to time, there will be stages in the continuum of eternity that are more or less near to its still centre, and whose position determines their degree of detachment from time, for only those aspects of time that have achieved perfection of form or essence in time are finally separated from time. Those that have not might have to be sieved again and again through time, until they have reached the final positiveness and spirituality of eternity. Time—God-made—uses all the virtualities and possibilities of being in time, so as to get for ever out of time. These possibilities are all, in varying degrees, connected with extension in space, and it could be only when time and space were reduced to spirit that time and eternity would be at one, and that there would no longer be any question of stages or positions more or less near to the still centre. Then perfect harmony would enfold all aspects of fully and perfectly actualised possibilities of time and perfectly self-knowing Being, which can only be Being if He creates, by separating Himself from Himself; therefore, this stage of absolute self-knowledge could no sooner be reached than it would be broken, and such is the simultaneousness of all things in eternity that it is never either reached or not reached, and there never is a transition either from the one to the other or vice-versa, so that the cycle of time and eternity, like a spiral without beginning or end, continues its eternal unfolding of creation as the eternal knowing and making of God.

The idea of God waiting for death to weigh individually every soul or spirit, to reward it or punish it according to its deserts, is irreconcilable with the idea of God as absolute Being and plenitude of all perfections. It merely turns Him

31

into the archetypal Accountant or Headmaster. Every man makes his own eternal essence, that is to say what he will finally be in eternity, through his own life. Every man is progressively sifted into his own final purity—or lack of it—in the same way as drinking water is sifted through processes that make it drinkable. The process is automatic and constant, and the final result is the outcome of the original essence (or DNA, for the materialists) and the circumstances through which it has lived and the way it has lived them. The human being naturally aspires to the divine, or if, through spiritual limitations or adverse social conditions in which he lives, he lacks such aspirations, he tends to deify himself. Man's inherent and essential longing is to transcend time and to outface death, either by connecting with the eternal forms or through absolute nothingness.

God is in man, whom He created, therefore He loves him and offers him everything, but does not compel him to accept anything. He leaves him free to choose and to discover by himself his truth, and by so doing, to be truly himself, free from all contingencies, which can have no weight whatsoever for the one who is aware of his true self as the essence which connects him with God or Being. Joy in life corresponds to awareness of the eternal in man, and pain corresponds to awareness of the weight of time which obnubilates spirit and reduces it to a piercing preoccupation with itself as pain. Pain is the negation of everything except itself, the reduction of life to a cry or an ache which fills and abolishes the mind. Pain ties us to time, but it can also take us out of it, if it is not overwhelming, for just as we know the true meaning and importance of a given love or affection only when we lose it or are about to lose it, in the same way, we reach metaphysical or ontological knowledge only through pain. Man must always go into the dark, the dark of pain, the dark of night, the dark of death, in order to be reborn to light.

2

The Sense of Guilt

The guilt feeling is above all the feeling of separation from the whole, the feeling of individuation and isolation from other subjects and from intersubjectivity, and therefore a feeling both of anguish and of longing to put an end to this separation. It is a feeling that is somehow always connected with the notion that something in us, or outside us, has caused this separation and this suffering, and that something or somebody is responsible for it. Eve, Adam and other myths and legends that explain man's fall from grace and primal bliss all aim at conveying the basic truth that separation from the whole, from the womb of life, or merely from the maternal womb, caused a fundamental traumatism, from which man can be cured only by death. We cannot bear our sense of guilt; there must always be someone to be blamed for it and to take its weight away from us; it must be either Christ, the new Adam, or people we love, and whom we tend to blame for our failures and short-comings. It is perhaps because of this that Nietzsche dismissed Christianity as a religion of the weak, a religion which encourages the notion that there is always some scapegoat ready to bear and to cleanse our guilt.

The notion of the scapegoat is, no doubt, something inherent in the concept of religion. In order to bind the human to the supernatural, there must be some sacrifice—animal, human or divine—like Dionysus, the archetypal founder of Greek tragedy in which the hero—Oedipus or Orestes—is the scapegoat carrying the sin of the community, eaten by it as a redeeming force; both Oedipus and Orestes are put to death, and acquire numinous powers after their death. Christianity has retained the notion that Christ-God sacrificed Himself to redeem man's guilt. Yet man is only what God made him, and therefore he can only be guilty of limitations inherent in his nature and not involving the Divine, which need not die for him in order to redeem him, but needs, on the contrary, to throw its light and love over him in order to illumine his earthly path. Man must bear his own burden, his own guilt by himself, for it is only by freely taking upon ourselves, and ourselves alone, our own guilt that we can free ourselves from it. We cannot wipe away our feeling of guilt through someone's sacrifice or sorrows; we must accept our own guilt ourselves, whatever type of guilt it is, without involving anyone else, human or divine. Man's sense of guilt on the metaphysical or ontological level can only be the feeling of isolation from the wholeness of creation, and the incapacity to maintain oneness with other members of it, and with the Creator, owing to his innate lack of the requisite means of doing so. Man is aware that he is a fragment, a divine fragment of the force that animates the universe, and he is aware that, as such, he can neither fully apprehend the reality of other fragments like himself nor, least of all, encompass the living reality of the whole, therefore he knows that he has to wait for the end of his own time on earth, and for the end of time itself, to be part of the self-knowing whole.

Creation necessarily entails a withdrawal of spirit or God so that it might come into existence. Man is aware of this lack, or withdrawal of spirit, and he longs for the fulfilment of this need, that is to say for a return to pure spirit. Creation is God's necessity, so that he may know Himself perfectly through existence and time, and God cannot look upon man without being aware of his limitations and his lack of a totality of spirit, and God, as pure spirit, cannot but be pained by any absence of spirit. Man, on the other hand, cannot look upon God without being pained and anguished by the awareness of his own limitations and by the distance that separates him from Him. He may hope or intuitively long to bridge this distance, through humility and divine Grace, but he can never hope to be able to conceive of it as bridgeable, because, being part of time, he cannot possibly conceive of eternity. He is condemned to dream of this concept, but he cannot give form to it and encompass it; his only experience of eternity is not through concepts at all, but through his total loss of awareness of self in mystical union with God or the eternal.

Creation is necessarily limitation and finitude, and some may call this original sin, something that death and the end of time redeem by returning the individual to the whole. 'Original sin', whatever it is, cannot be the result of any act of so-called free will, for there cannot be any act of free will, either regarding the birth of creation or Adam's choice as to what to do or not to do. To think that God might not have willed creation is to think of God as absolutely perfect, totally still and self-contained, and therefore, in fact, not creative, but involved in a state of absolute self-contemplation, from which the notion of love would be totally excluded, since there would be nothing but the pure transparency of Himself, and nothing to receive and return His love. Therefore God without creation would be non-God or non-Being, a contradiction in terms. If God in order to be God could not avoid creating, then the act of creation could not be a matter of one moment rather than another—something that would involve the notion of free will and choice, but purely a question of such an act taking place at the optimum moment, that is to say at the moment that is the only one and the best as seen by God's all-knowing mind. There is no possible reason to think that God either could body forth creation at a moment which was not the best and only moment, or that He could hesitate, through ignorance or lack of will, as to when this optimum moment was. So that, given God's attributes of perfect goodness, love, omniscience and omnipotence, creation can only be a necessary act, in the sense that it could neither fail to be, nor be at any other time than the one at which it was, that is, no time at all, since time can have neither beginning nor end, so that creation is coeval with God.

Adam and Eve, being part of this necessity, could not be conceived as being able to be taken out of it and endowed with a spark of the notion which is supposed to be free will, or rather, they could, if one wishes, be so imagined, as part of a game that God could have chosen to play, but, as Einstein said, God does not play games, either with dice or any other instruments. He is and can only be absolute necessity, a necessity which subsumes all perfections, including, naturally, the notion of free will as part of the basic notion that God cannot but always do the best, so that the best which He necessarily knows and practises, which is also His free will, is the only course He can take without falling short of the total perfection which is His and which, if this happened, would make of Him something less than God. The metaphysical notion of sin does not exist; it is an illusion, and it can be disposed of only by being recognised as an illusion inherent in time, and which the awareness of true being dispels, or transmutes into the reality of its own positiveness. On the contrary, the awareness of one's own non-existence or non-being—an awareness one may have when one denies true love or true goodness—is the cause of a suffering which lasts until one accepts their vital reality and, by so doing, proves that one is fully aware that they truly are the essence and aim of life. If one loses the awareness that life necessarily entails suffering and that man must accept suffering as part of it, and transcend it through his faith in the positiveness and purposefulness of life and in the supreme wisdom of its unfolding as part of creation, then life can become a burden, or a source of revolt against its incomprehensibility, for those who have to endure it in such a lack of light.

Suffering cannot always be mastered and accepted; far from it, it is very often unbearable. The body is very often torn and overwhelmed by pain, as Christ's was at the point of death, so that his cry of anguish echoes the time-long cry of mankind at the impossibility of understanding suffering and death. The body has its laws, which the spirit, however strong, cannot always control, and in moments of great pain all other forms of consciousness disappear except that of pain, so that the whole of life, spiritual and material, turns into pain, and man ceases to be man and is reduced to a cry of despair or a plea that this despair may stop at last. This is the cry of Christ: 'My God, my God, why hast thou forsaken me?'—and God did not answer, any more than He answers when He is asked by a despairing mother: 'Why this death, why this suffering?' He does not answer, for there is nothing He could say. He could not explain the death of a child, or the indifferent suffering of the innocent as well as the wicked; no explanation is possible, except that suffering and death are part of life, like the seasons, the budding and falling of leaves, the birth and death of butterflies and of everything that is involved in creation. All these things must be accepted as part of the harmony of life, with its multi-coloured patches, as part of the faith in the wisdom of God whose silence tells man to accept what comes to him with courage and faith in creation, for by so doing he unites himself with Him and accepts the order of things, an order which is God's *nous*, including our limitations, our suffering, as well as the joy of total reunion with Him. The cross of Christ makes it clear to man that there cannot be any creation without suffering and death, and that they must be accepted as Christ accepted them, and accepts them still, by sharing every man's suffering and death.

True love is the love of the other; and truth itself, that is to say, of course, the truth of experience, is only truth in relation to the absolute of otherness which is God. The capacity to suffer with the other, through the awareness that the other is also ourselves and that we are one and the same with him, is the archetype of all virtues, symbolised by the life of Christ and that of the saints, and by the transposition, through pure love, of oneself into another, so as to share with him his suffering and sorrows. It implies the spontaneous, non-willed merging of one *I* with another, so as to help him to bear his burden. This can take place only if one thinks oneself absolutely worthless by oneself, and as being valuable only in relation to one's capacity to serve others. The *I* is thus not the *I* for itself, but an *I* for others, and it is in the urge to be an *I* for others, which is the opposite of the egotistical, that the possibility of social well-being lies, of love and respect for other men, and of total devotion to truth.

The intrusion of the self destroys every human value and ties us down to La Rochefoucauld's philosophy which is ruthlessly clear-eyed about this most basic human failing. As he puts it, 'one always has enough strength to bear other people's affliction', and we bear it because we experience a sense of comfort at being spared it, and a sense of gratification at the sight of suffering which could be ours, but is not ours. La Rochefoucauld's age was dominated by the Cartesian *I*, foundation of all things, including the awareness of existence itself. Still, lest one might be tempted to look upon historical epochs as composed of single cohorts marching unswervingly under a single flag, let us not forget Pascal with his famous 'le moi est

37

haïssable', and also the widespread importance of mysticism in France as well as in England and Spain at that time.

The will, the *I* in action is the enemy of the good, the true, and of art itself. It can only cause corruption of essences and distortions to suit the ego. The good cannot tolerate the will, and any willed good is not good, but an action performed with a purpose and end in view. The purpose in view may be to conform with the image one has of the good, the end could very well be self-satisfaction. Will therefore corrupts the good, as vinegar corrupts good wine; either the good action is perfectly spontaneous, without forethought or afterthought, or it is not good, even though it may not be without some social worth, for even crooked good is better than no good. A beggar would rather receive a warm meal or a cloak, even if the gesture is made for purely egotistical ends, than be turned away in the cold. If one does good without thinking and if, later, one thinks that such an action has been good, one takes some of the good out of it, for one might be led to derive some self-satisfaction and pride from it. Awareness of the good has exactly the same effect on it as Orpheus had on Eurydice when they were walking out of the Underworld: his hasty gaze confined her for ever to the shades.

3

Good and Evil

The essence of creation contains both the positive and the negative, and all aspects of life are dialectical, that is to say compounded of opposites and dissymmetries, which resolve themselves into harmonies. Absolute goodness is no more thinkable than absolute evil, absolute freedom or chance. Absolute, all-embracing goodness would exclude creation, which is the making of perfection through time, and which can only be at the cost of a limitation of goodness, or of a partial lack of goodness, generally described as evil. Creation is only possible through God's wilful and necessary acceptance of imperfection, and without it, it is no more possible than life would be possible if the earth were not far enough removed from the intense heat of the sun. Everything of the earth must necessarily 'fall short of God's glory', must necessarily be short of goodness, of wisdom and knowledge, and therefore, up to a point, must always be stained with evil, as a kind, if one wishes, of original sin. This sin will be all the greater if man, lacking in humility and in the awareness of his enduring limitations, arrogates to himself a knowledge or power which can belong only to God; that is to say, if he tries, as stated in *Genesis*, 'to become as one of us, to know good and evil'.

Man has a more or less acute awareness of good and evil; yet, whatever he does, he can never achieve perfect goodness, and evil, unknown to him, lurks, at times, in his best intentions. God or Being is part of creation in varying degrees. Some aspects of creation have, in essence, a greater awareness of God than others; therefore they are nearer to Him than others, and they require less of His attention and grace to sustain them through life, and to be finally brought to Him. The less essence a human being has, the less he is aware of God and of true goodness, the more of God's goodness he requires, so as to be brought to Him. The evil man necessarily requires more attention than the good man, who is nearer to God. This does not mean that God loves the evil man more than the good man, for that would be an intolerable paradox which would give greater value to evil than to goodness. It means that God has to supply more love to sustain an evil man alive, so as to give him the possibility of redeeming himself in time, than He has to do in order to sustain alive a good man, who, being so, has already redeemed himself and is therefore already fit for God's presence, through death, at any time. On the human plane, it means that it takes more humility, more goodness, to countenance and to integrate evil than it takes to help a good man. Thus, evil itself is a means through which value can be achieved, but it is not a value in itself, while on the contrary goodness is, whatever the concrete application it may receive, or the uses it may be put to.

Evil is the distance between creation and the Creator, between man and God, and the greater the distance, the greater the effort required to bring the two together, as they must be, for they are one and the same, separated by time— Christ's passion—through which existence redeems itself and returns to essence. Christ-God will suffer as long as creation, and he suffers all the more because some aspects of creation are afflicted with more evil than others, are more remote from Him and thus require more love to be lifted into the purity of essence. The greater the cold, that is to say the greater the distance between God and man, the greater the fire of God's love, in order to consume the object which requires it, and which, once refined, returns to its source and contributes to the restoration of the broken equilibrium of the eternal.

No man can help being conscious of evil, within himself and in others. Evil is part of man's innate limitations as a finite being, and it must be accepted as part of the great mystery of life which Christ's life and death unfold like a book for us to read and to follow. Every man has to endure his suffering, his sorrows and his death, by himself, and in the end in solitude, with only the light of his faith, and confident that, since Christ-God accepted all before him, and continuously accepts it side by side with him and with his fellow-beings, until the end of creation, this is the only way. Christ's disciples slept when he needed their love and help, and God, his Father, remained silent when the bitterness of death was for one moment too much for him and when he prayed in agony and doubt: 'O my Father, if it be possible, let this cup pass from me.' It did not; he understood, and, then and for ever, he accepted God's will, as must all men.

Christ is creation, and his life and death are God's light to illumine man's way and to show him the reality of his relationship with Him. Christ was not born, like Adam, in Eden; he was born in difficult circumstances, amongst a subjugated people. He knew the loneliness of desert nights and the solitude of suffering, and whether he cured palsy or leprosy, which were then described as sins, or forgave the sins of sinners, it was always in the name of faith and the love of God. His death is an example which all men must follow, and his story of the two debtors shows both that he frankly forgave both, and that it is through faith that the individual is regenerated and reborn: Luke VII, 37–50.

'Man', said Victor Hugo, 'writes his destiny, day after day, in thick black ink; at the same time, God writes in between the lines in invisible ink.' Life, as someone put it, is a tapestry; God sees the final, perfectly finished side, man sees only the obverse, full of loose threads, knots and holes, and cannot understand or guess the perfection and beauty of the other side. The perfection of creation, for us, is like the dark side of the moon, we can never see it, unless we go to the moon or unless we ourselves pass to the other side, where there is nothing hidden and where God's invisible light becomes finally visible. As finite beings, we can only grasp fragmentary aspects of life, like diamonds embedded in coal, which give us only a very faint idea of what the pure diamond of truth could be. 'Everything here on earth', said Pascal, 'is partly true and partly false; but essential truth is not like this, it is totally pure and true. The mixture we find here on earth both dishonours and destroys truth.' (*Les Pensées*, ed. Brunschvicg, Hachette, p. 504) 'How could it be possible for a part to know the whole? Man may perhaps aspire to the knowledge of at least those parts of the world which are on the same scale as himself, but these are

41

so closely linked and related together that I hold it to be impossible to know one without knowing the other and without knowing the whole.' (Pascal, ibid., p. 355)

From Plato's mediation of the truth through the Idea, to Augustine's mediation of the truth through God, Hegel's through the Absolute or Marx's through the totality of history, truth is, from all accounts, only apprehensible through the whole. The individual can be understood only as part of a greater whole—society, civilisation, history or time, and he can know himself only in relation to these various wholes, each of which is a set of relationships between its component parts. This is Hegel's as well as Marx's view, and neither ignores, as is sometimes suggested, the importance of the individual by submerging him into the whole, which, according to both, can be understood only in terms of the totality of the individuals composing it. Then the contradictions or dialectics of life are resolved, into the Absolute for the one, and in the New Jerusalem for the other, that is to say, in the end, in the ideal world. Thus in Marxism the future, tomorrow and not-Being provide the context that gives meaning and purpose to individual life and to the present, and the future is being made by man who, of course, can interpret it according to his own dreams and desires. God also makes or rather completes His own perfection and total self-knowledge by actualising His positive virtualities in creation which responds to His love by loving Him in return and thus closes the circle between Himself and His creation as His self-expression. The incarnation underlines the belief that everything in life is informed with God's essence and stresses as much as Hegel or Marx the importance of time and history, but the New Jerusalem of the Christian world is reached not so much by Marxist marches and countermarches between dialectically opposed politico-social systems as by the capacity to shed the contingent and to give spiritual values the place they ought to occupy in time and consequently beyond time.

The example of saints like St Francis or St François de Sales shows that action plays a vital part in the implementation of faith. Above all, the life of Christ, a life of action, surrounded by artisans, themselves men of action, makes this point very clear. Body and mind, matter and spirit are one and cannot be dissociated. Christ lived and worked among very plain men, but when he needed to find his truth and to listen to the voice of God so as to muster the forces he would need to carry out his spiritual tasks, he withdrew to the desert for forty days and forty nights. Moses climbed Mount Sinai to listen to the voice of God, and St John of the Cross and Pascal found Him in their night of illumination. In truth, they did not set out to find Him; God found them, as He found St Francis and St Teresa of Avila. In religion as well as in art, pursuit leads nowhere, or rather, wherever it may lead, it is not to religion or art, for which, as Shakespeare admirably put it, 'the readiness is all'. The same point about happiness is made by La Fontaine in his fable 'Les Deux Pigeons', in which the one who has gone away in search of happiness finally returns home battered by fatigue, winds and rain, to find happiness quietly waiting on his doorstep. God calls those who are ready to hear Him and to receive Him, and He may sometimes have to call many times, for people have other noises in their heads. But they will hear Him only if they listen, and they will find Him not if they search for Him, but if they prepare themselves and wait for His coming, for the more we move, the more difficult it is for someone who is looking for us to find us, while if we can stand still, the chances for us to be found are increased by half. In the end, wisdom is waiting, not roaming about or trying to grasp what cannot be grasped.

Creation separates God from God, and man from God, in as far as man is creation incarnated in time. The separating element is matter informed with energy and coeval with it, but confined to extensions in space, while energy and spirit are not. Matter, therefore, is both informed with essence and also, because of its own laws, appetites and finality, it constitutes a screen standing in the way of the truth of essence. It is a disguise, an alibi behind which the soul or spirit avoids its responsibility, which is readiness to know and to connect with essence. The incapacity to attend to and recognise essence is due to our listening to the demand for the satisfactions of matter or the flesh, and our refusal to turn our gaze in the direction which would make it possible for us to receive essence or to recognise it. The body is man, but man is not only body, he is also spirit, therefore, though the body must have its say, it must do so without stifling the spirit; for if we are only bodies intent upon satisfying our appetites, our ambitions and our egoisms, we have no chance whatsoever of being made aware of the reality of life and of its finality which is the fulfilment of its timeless essence.

Matter by itself cannot be said to be evil except as part of a simplistic manicheism which seeks to apportion to it all human failings. Matter is perfectly obedient to God's laws, therefore perfectly lovable, whatever shape it takes; flowers, trees, the seas and the animal world in its naturalness are all beautiful. Matter is also beautiful in art, when it has not been raped or egotistically moulded in response to selfish aims, but when, on the contrary, its essence has been respected and has been made to blend with the essence of genius so as to create analogies of divine beauty and harmony, when, in fact, it has become a vessel, a symbol to embody eternal truth. Such truths, such harmonies can only be achieved if all contradictions have been abolished, all evils, if evil there is, resolved into the positiveness of the good, for the good is not the good by itself, but is as much an abolition and a resolution of evil into the pure positiveness of perfect love, as a light is a dispersion and destruction of all darkness.

The truth of essence can be reached only through individuated essence in a state of perfect receptivity and will-lessness that makes possible its union with Essence or Being. Such moments are rare and they can never be achieved through will, for conscious will is always will to something which is not truth or pure goodness, but the fulfilment of a desire, an urge or a need, imposed by the ego, and therefore opposed to intersubjectivity and to the receptivity of anything except the demands or dictations of the ego. The individual will on its own is merely a manifestation of egotistical desires and instincts, which are isolating and not all-embracing or aware of the other. The will on its own is separated from the whole, therefore from the absolute good which it is not aware of, and, by so being, it is unaware of its essence or goodness, for the good is not individual but universal, and the individual good is either related to it or it is not truly good. The will is free only when liberated from all impediments related to the self, or from finitude, and united as essence with God's essence or will which is the will to perfect goodness, beauty and eternal truth; it is only free when it can say with Dante: 'La sua voluntate è nostra pace'. (*Paradiso*, Canto 3)

True consciousness is annihilation of the self and awareness of the individual will as God's will. The individual will has no power to bring about salvation or, for that matter, artistic creation, which is a spontaneous upsurge of being intent upon its own finality. Wilfulness in art can only produce inferior art. Art is not reproduction of appearances, but incarnation of essences, primarily carried out in a state of receptiveness reached through humility and some kind of grace, born from the reverence which the artist must have for his creativity. The model, schema or guiding light is the vision of what the creative mind is trying to bring to life, a vision which is not a thing, but a living force shaping itself into harmonised forms which embody it as truth. The artist listens and translates the transcendent, the invisible, into apprehensible signs; he reveals the truth or essence of things, and he does this by relating his own essence to that of the thing to be known, through the Divine, source of all essences, and mediating between them. It would be impossible for man to know anything of the reality of things, unless there were an essence underlying this reality, shared both by nature and by man, and constituting both the order and the finality of the world.

Truth cannot be reduced to the intellect. Mathematical and logical truth, which rests upon axioms and principles, may be accepted or rejected according to whether the calculations or arguments based upon them pass or do not pass the agreed tests. Physical laws can be verified by experimentation, but the truth of experience can be verified only by life apprehended subjectively, and it is universally true irrespective of time, place and the appearances or topical emphases which it exhibits. The knowledge of experience or wisdom—the knowledge of the philosopher, the poet or the artist—is not basically a matter of wilful pursuit and interpretations; it is, like faith, primarily a matter of will-lessness and receptivity so that the individuated self might connect with intersubjectivity or the unconscious where the truth of human experience has lain since man became man. Rationality is no more excluded from such an operation than it is excluded from the Thomistic or Pascalian approach to faith; it can prepare the ground, and above all it must unfold or organise into artistic or logical coherence the apprehensions of the original vision, but it cannot make the leap which connects individuated essence with being, it cannot be the electric current which, when positive and negative meet, immediately causes light, heat and revelation of truth. The truths thus revealed are part of the unconscious or inter-subjectivity, and are images or archetypes which embody perennial structures of suffering, sorrows or joys, fears, longings, which men have undergone and will undergo until the end of time. Every human consciousness carries, in varying degrees, glimpses which, like half-dead embers, could be revived into fires, if and when they became connected with their living source which is man's subconscious. Revelations of truth through art or through philosophy at its highest, as with Plato, Pascal, Hegel, Kant, Schopenhauer or Nietzsche, transcend the age when they were brought to life and connect the past with the present, by bringing into consciousness truths that are not only part of the age when they emerged, but part of the life of mankind.

The will as controlled by the conscious *I* can transform matter, raise or flatten mountains, unpeople cities and destroy part of mankind, but it has no effect whatever upon the spiritual. The will does not have the power to bring anyone nearer to God or to true love. All *effort* to reach God or true love is of no avail, for God or love can only come, not when or where there is a will to meet them, but when and where there is readiness to receive them. This readiness requires more exertions of self-preparation than are required by the kinetic manifestations of the conscious will.

True love is not a matter of pursuits and sieges. This concept of love, dear to Stendhal, Laclos and all those who look upon it as an intellectual game, or a Chamfortian contact of two epidermises, has really nothing to do with love, which is a recognition of the other as belonging to the same being as oneself. Love as a pursuit, as a hunt, is part of the master-slave, hunter-hunted relationship between man and woman. It posits a sadistic climate and a power complex which urges the male animal to dominate his female quarry. This is not love, but cannibalism or crude eroticism—an ancient ritual of transmutation which has become part of a civilisation that bases its values on wealth and power, and not on true love and human brotherhood. Woman is merely one of the pleasures of a hedonistic, power-ridden society, worshipping strength in all its forms, and in which woman, having the excuse of millennia of domination, still allows and welcomes the exploitation of herself for purely material ends.

Wilfulness is totally alien to the greatest values of mankind. Neither love nor beauty nor happiness nor, least of all, Being can be approached through will. All these things can come to man only as if through an act of grace, that is to say as something given without asking, for to ask is to conjure away or to destroy. The poet who sits down at his table saying to himself 'I will write a poem' may, if he has mastered enough technique, write some ode or epigram, but he will not write *Kubla Khan* or *Ode to a Nightingale*. The moment Psyche's impatience drove her too close for safety to sleeping Cupid, and she thus awakened him, love fled away, never to return. As Valéry put it:

> Patience, patience,
> Patience dans l'azur!
> Chaque atome de silence
> Est la chance d'un fruit mûr!   (*Palme*)

Love of one's fellow beings must be constantly practised without any postponement to tomorrow, or attempts to pass one's responsibility on to another. The Good Samaritan did not wait for the sun's rays to warm up the naked body of his fellow man; he gave him, at once, half of his cloak. Christian life is action and not progressive elimination or refusal of action as in Buddhism, nor is it, of course, action for action's sake, as if it were some kind of St Vitus's dance, but action in order to fulfil God's law, which is to bring about the maximum amount of good in creation. Christianity, in the wake of Christ's example, is essentially devoted to the divinising of matter through physical and spiritual activity. This activity should affect all spheres of life—the street as well as the home, the factory as well as the church, for a religion that is confined to a church is merely empty ritual practice on the fringe of life, without any effect on it. Religion is man's innate aspiration

47

towards spiritualisation through the love which unites him to his fellow beings and to his Creator, and through his understanding of the true purpose and meaning of life. It is an activity which should inform the whole of life, so that man, whatever he does, is always conscious of his responsibility towards his fellow beings and towards himself as part of creation.

4

Death

Our circle narrows with each passing day;
One's in the grave; one wanders far away;
Beneath fate's glance we fade; the days speed by.
                              Pushkin: '19th October'

Man is part of creation, therefore part of Christ's crucifixion
which is coeval with time, so that suffering and death must be
looked upon as necessary parts of life. Every human being is the
image of Christ and, like him, has his cross to bear. God Himself
is, as previously outlined, necessary both in His essence and in
whatever He does, including His creation. The only response
to necessity is obedience, which is part of it, for, in the end, one
can neither reject necessity nor alter it; one can only give
oneself the illusion of doing so, an illusion which might give
one a feeling of revolt and self-satisfied stoic pride, but which
merely consists in shouting 'no' to the wind or, like King
Canute, in trying to stem the tide with one's bare hands. Job's
truth carries no other lesson than that necessity, which is
inherent in essence, entails obedience to it, through the
recognition that it is so and that one cannot change it. This
does not mean that the human being can always manage to
accept suffering with equanimity, if not with joy. He can only
do so if his spirit is not broken by physical pain; when in such
states, and unfortunately they happen often enough, he ceases
to be a true human being and he becomes a broken-down
animal, temporarily disconnected from being and, at the
conscious level, from God, and he thus is reduced to oscillating
between abject abasement and longing for death and for the
dark in his moments of lucidity and hopelessness about his fate.

49

These moments of lucidity—flashes of lightning in a dark night—are all the more harrowing because the mind knows pain only through compulsion, and therefore resists it to its utmost, for its essence is to be free and not to be fettered by the flesh or by the body in pain. So that, in such moments, there is a struggle between the mind as awareness of the body, and the mind as freedom wanting to separate itself from the body and to reject the body which inflicts such abasement upon it. This feeling of abasement can be known only through experience, for it involves such a total interdependence between body and spirit that imagination alone, unfed by experience which moulds it and expresses itself through it, could not by itself reach the truth of this reality. Without experience, imagination runs the risk of turning into an abstraction, or a purely intellectual concept, an aspect of existential reality which is of ontological dimension. The essence of mind being freedom, its tendency is to ignore the body and to try to turn, if it is possible, the pressures of harrowing bodily pain into all sorts of illusions so as to avoid the effort of facing it or transcending it, or being overwhelmed by it. Yet suffering can only be transcended, as long as the mind retains the strength to do so, through conscious recognition of the fact that it is part of life, in the same way as death itself is part of life, and thus must be accepted as a stark reality implying the total break-up of our physical organism and its separation from essence which, while we have life, we know nothing of, and which is so awesome that it cannot be contemplated without terror, unless life has been a long preparation for it.

To live is to learn how to die, and one does not truly live if one does not practise this most difficult discipline so as to learn how to face this final and most important stage of life. Wisdom consists in learning how to muster the necessary obedience to face and to accept death. Yet that is more easily said than done, for everything is against it, and Christ himself was unable to master his terror at the last moment, even though he knew that he was in his Father's hands, and that he himself was his own Father, since he was God. But the conflict between the existential and the eternal, at the point where the one had become fully and only the other, was too much even for him,

50

and he gave voice to his suffering, though not to despair, for he knew, or at least his inner self or essence knew, that life was elsewhere. In his worst moment of solitude and suffering, he had to bear all by himself, making clear the lesson that man must not only bear his suffering by himself, but also know that he suffers, and that he must accept it. This is the greatest test for man, and therefore there is no greater love than that which is genuinely and spontaneously directed to a suffering man in order to share and to lighten his burden. This love is the love of man's essence, the love of Christ, and thus the love of the Creator. It is a homage to life, for it helps the sufferer to pass from the stage of being an object overwhelmed by pain, to being again a subject connected with and part of life. This is the image of creation, necessarily entailing suffering which can be redeemed only by love that reunites creation with God. But the vital point to understand is that these necessary aspects of creation like suffering and death must be accepted without being mentally shunned or covered up under all kinds of disguises, for that is to live a life of bad faith and illusions, which will not, in the end, conjure away the reality of death.

The truth of life rests upon the acceptance of the cross, which he who wishes to live life in constant contact with reality must always keep to the forefront of his mind. There was no answer to Christ's 'Why hast thou forsaken me?', for there cannot be any in this world, which is what it is, with a causality and a finality which cannot be within the grasp of man, who is only a fragment of it and not the whole. God can no more answer our irate or anxious questioning than He answered Christ, for there is no possible answer except silence, and Christ did not alter his love, for he understood that he himself was the answer to himself and to man's age-long question. God's words are written on silence at this most crucial point of Christ's life, and at all moments of life, for whatever we do brings into play His silent judgment which we shall only be able to hear when time ceases deafening our ears and leaves us earless and eyeless to enjoy His eternal music and shadowless light. Man himself will not find the meaning of life written in fiery letters in the sky, he can only find the meaning of his joys and sorrows in his heart, and nowhere else, as long as he belongs to the earth and to time. Time is the cross of the spirit, which lies fragmented and dispersed through it, and will only be redeemed and restored to oneness by time's end. Then, all conflicts, all contrasts and oppositions will be resolved. Life as a whole tends towards order and equilibrium, and every disturbance in it has to be compensated for by its opposite or its complement, and through the rise and fall of the seasons, through continuous living and continuous dying, life pursues its ceaseless unfolding and change. Only the Eternal, or God, is unchanging in His essence. As Valéry says:

> Midi là-haut, midi sans mouvement
> En soi se pense et se convient à soi-même. . . .
> Tête complète et parfait diadème,
> Je suis en toi le secret changement.

The eternal is noonday, thinking itself, in perfect equilibrium within itself. Creation, the becoming of eternity, is change, continuous change, necessary to eternity, for light implies darkness:

> . . . mais rendre la lumière
> Suppose d'ombre une morne moitié

and the perfection of the eternal implies perfection reached through the becoming of living and dying, otherwise it would be the perfection of absolute death or non-being, a perfection which would be a non-perfection, since non-being can only be the negation of being, and not an entity endowed with an *ens* of non-being—something that is a contradiction in terms. Existence is being-for-an-end, which is death, as part of being in time. Death therefore is a necessary part of life, which, as life-for-death, can only be lived fully and wisely as a preparation for the unavoidable finality of death. Death begins with birth, which contains it as its finality, and if death is the finality of life, it stands to reason that it is the most important moment of life and the one which determines the true finality of individuated life as part of the eternal. Our death is only our beginning, the beginning of what we shall be for ever. Therefore, it is of the utmost importance, for those who hold this belief, that they should be fully aware of death throughout their lives, starting as soon as consciousness makes this possible.

Those who look upon organic life as a pure aggregate of matter cannot have such preoccupations, and they lead their lives according to values which have no transcendental connotations, and which are, on the whole, more or less contingent to individual judgment, circumstances, time and place. The acceptance of the notion that life is for death, however unjust or incomprehensible this may at times appear to be, is the most important factor of human destiny. It gives life its tragic dimension; it lifts it up out of the contingent, the absurd, the inconsequential, and, above all, away from the superficial stoicism of those who profess not to believe in the Divine and yet adopt a pose of disdain or revolt that posits, as a background against which to revolt, a notion of the Divine to which the human is easily superior through his courage, suffering and death. Such an attitude may be exhilarating for the weak, and comforting for those who wish to strike heroic or singular attitudes, but it is as barren as a philosophy of life as it is for human brotherhood, for, in spite of its profession of faith about fraternity and human love, it can only lead, with rare exceptions, to hedonism practised by monadic entities wrapped up in their isolation, from which they surge forth every now and then, prompted by the pleasure principle or by the demands of their ego. In such a context, death can be looked upon either as something distasteful, which must be got over like a nasty medicine, or with the calm indifference of stoic philosophers who choose their own moment of death as they choose the moment to go to the barber's shop or to the baths. Such a death has a certain nobility, the nobility of courage and acceptance, but it lacks the dimension of wisdom and of the sense of tragedy that gives meaning to life. To die bravely at the moment of one's choosing, or in battle, is a way that lacks neither grandeur nor virtue, but it is a way that nevertheless obfuscates the true face of death behind a given value—free will or patriotism—which takes away its meaning and deprives it of its value and finality as the maker of eternity. Ontological truth is replaced by contingent, man-made values transmuted onto the plane of the eternal. To will one's death, in one way or another, is to assume that one can impose a human will or choice upon eternity; and that is not possible. If, on the other hand, one does not believe in eternity, Yeats's poem on the death of an airman is the most appropriate way of describing such a gratuitous gesture lacking neither in elegance nor in impressiveness, yet completely disconnected from the aura of transcendence and necessity that pertains to an order of things in which life and death have their true meaning as an integral part of it:

> A lonely impulse of delight
> Drove to this tumult in the clouds;
> I balanced all, brought all to mind,
> The years to come seemed waste of breath,
> A waste of breath the years behind
> In balance with this life, this death.

A death which is given a motivation or a contingent meaning is no longer a tragic death—part of necessity and transcendence. To choose it, as in the case of consciously chosen suicide, is to make of it a human tool, to debase it to the human level, while tragic death must, through its incomprehensibility, be part of the divine order, whose becoming necessarily entails death as well as life. The tragic hero always died without knowing why, and at the hands of fate, for it was only in such a way that he himself could posthumously become a value for the society to which he belonged. The human being knows that he will never solve the mystery of death; all he can do is to give it a meaning which is adequate to his beliefs, all tending, in one way or another, to dispose of the uncontrollable fear that seizes him in the face of the total and final loss of consciousness and individual identity.

To declare that suffering and death are absurd is to assume, through such a judgment, an attitude of superiority and knowingness over the order of nature and life which may bring some cold comfort to those who need it, but contributes nothing to the understanding of the true meaning of life. Besides that, it marks a flight from humility which is the only attitude that man could reasonably adopt in the face of the mystery of life and death. To say that either is absurd means that one has been able to ascertain its scope and reality, and to come to the conclusion that there is no meaning in it; therefore by so doing, one places oneself in the God-like position of being able to define what cannot be defined, not even at the level of God Himself, Who only knows Himself in totality through the becoming of being which is the informing essence of creation. Suffering and death can neither be understood nor spirited away under the label of 'absurd'. They are a part of life, and they must be accepted as such, and integrated in human consciousness which, through such acceptance, transcends them. The wisest men—saints, philosophers and other geniuses —prepare for them, from the moment they begin being conscious of them. As genius is, above all, awareness of essence, it is made very early aware of the unavoidability of death and of the tragic sense of life. Mozart, Keats, Rimbaud did not wait for old age, which they never reached, to be aware of Blake's vision of life:

> O Rose, thou art sick!
> The invisible worm
> That flies in the night,
> In the howling storm,
>
> Has found out thy bed
> Of crimson joy,
> And his dark secret love
> Does thy life destroy.

This invisible worm is also Valéry's:

> Le vrai rongeur, le ver irréfutable
> N'est point pour vous qui dormez sous la table,
> Il vit de vie, et ne me quitte pas!

It is part of the rose that is life, and, in the end, it will have its say, so that the only thing that man can do is to prepare for the coming of this final moment which gives access to a world in which truth and beauty are eternally one.

Evil and death cannot be understood without Christ's sacrifice. God would not be God without the Crucifixion,

55

which is the only answer to age-long human cries against unjust suffering and untimely death. It is God's way of testifying to His love for man, by accepting, like him, suffering and death in human shape. Death is the great riddle which no human mind or religion has ever been able to solve. Scientific knowledge can tell us what it is, but not why it has to be so; thus making it irrevocably clear that knowledge and belief are two very different things and that, though they may at times coincide, the one cannot replace the other. Science's supreme value is truth. Yet, what is truth? The truth that two and two make four?—mere convention! The truth of the senses?—an infinite source of distortions and disagreements! The truth of the laws of nature?—certainly, for they are both verifiable and repeatable. But what about moral truth? What about the unverifiable truth of faith? No wonder one of Dostoyevsky's characters says: 'If I were compelled to choose between Christ and truth, I should choose to stay with Christ, against truth', and rightly so, for Christ is pure love, therefore truth, the only truth that brings to man a light and a balm for his suffering and his anxiety-ridden heart. The knowledge that $E = Mc^2$ could neither make St Martin share his cloak with a beggar nor teach this same beggar how to die, and die he must. Whatever the range of the knowledge it provides, science—the dream of learning and of better tomorrows through knowledge—is only a dream in which the saint and the holy man are replaced by the man in white overalls in front of his blackboard, and the hand that upholds and heals by the finger that points the way. We pass from a world of candles and glowing light to an antiseptic world of dazzling white, in which symbols and abstract figures move to the music of mathematics, towards the perfect silence of the frozen earth. The fateful truth of death can never be taught. The living can never conceive what death truly is; the dead can't either. The words carved on countless tombstones: 'I was as you are; you will be as I am', are a repeated slap in the face to rationality and scepticism. This tormenting equation can neither be solved nor disposed of by mathematical calculations or a conjuror's sleight of hand. From the moment reflection dawned upon him, man has been hounded by irreducible anxiety fed by daily death. Neither the Greek Elyseum nor Buddhist nirvana and metempsychosis nor the

Christian Heaven has ever been able to dispose of the leaden weight of the corpse, eternally tied to man, as Mazeppa to his riding horse. This ontological partnership will last until time ceases to be time and becomes one with Eternity.

5

The Tragic Sense of Life

Tragedy does *not* teach 'resignation'—To represent terrible and questionable things is in itself an instinct for power and magnificence in an artist: he does not fear them—There is no such thing as pessimistic art—Art affirms. Job affirms.

Nietzsche: *The Will to Power*

Beauty is universal; it is an emanation of Being which informs creation at all times and places; therefore all the beautiful things of the world that were created before Christianity and all those that are created outside Christianity partake of Christianity and are Christian, in as far as Christ is an inherent part of creation. Heraclitus, Plato, Socrates are Christian, and the Parthenon, the Pyramids and the brotherly love of Buddha for his fellow beings are Christian, Christ having been in man since Adam—God-created, therefore bearing Christ's presence. An aborigine of Australia, knowing nothing about Christian religion, is as much Christ-bearing as a Judean or a Roman, for, though he is ignorant of his origin and destiny, the time will come when in this world or in the next he will know both. For the time being, he lives his life according to his means, and though he is far away from Jerusalem, the existence of which means nothing to him, he will, in due course, know positively or negatively what the New Jerusalem is. Christianity cannot be bound by the Christian Church; it overflows before, all around it and after it, and it embraces all men who in their own way are able to grasp and to practise the truth of Christ, the love of other men and the love of beauty which unites matter with spirit and dreams of a world of total spiritual brotherhood in the love of the Maker.

Christianity transcends its institutionalisations and is basically a matter of Christian virtues which can be present in men at all times and places. The cannibalism of pagan tribes and societies is not worse than the cannibalism of so-called Christian Victorian England or France, where it was practised at one remove. All men are God's creatures, and the cross, Christ's presence, embraces all men from the first to the last, from the Israelis to the Indians, from the Chinese and the Eskimos to the Germans, who lately did such injury to Christ, or the Russians who continue to do so by peopling Gulag Archipeligos with suffering, Christ-bearing men. All men are more or less near to God, according to the way they reflect His light, and not according to their professions of faith or institutional attachments. It is not possible to conceive of a God Who, out of a human kind extending over more than half a million years, including approximately six thousand years of civilisation, could have decided to consider as His own children only those who, during the last two thousand years, have belonged to a church that nominally does not embrace any more than a quarter or so of mankind. Such exclusiveness and favouritism could not be reconcilable with the idea of God's eternal goodness. For God, all men, whether born in the fourth millennium BC on the banks of the Euphrates, or in the sixth century BC on the Attic shores, are equal in His eyes, but just as the saint, because of his constant awareness of God's presence in himself and in all aspects of life, and because of his constant attention to God's laws, is nearer to God than the average man, so the Christian of Florence or Rome is nearer to God than Hamilcar Barca's Cartheginians, because God's presence manifests itself through the Holy Eucharist and not through yearly Molochian sacrifices of children.

Man can only come to recognise God slowly and progressively, through time and the slow maturation of the mind. At the beginning, man-child was concerned only with his needs and self-interests, but progressively, through the growth of his mind, he has been able to detach himself from nature and the supernatural, and to listen to the voice of his widening conscience which tells him that other men are not his enemies but his brothers, and that the force to which he owes life is neither placated nor increased by human sacrifices, for this force is love, and, just as light can be increased only by more light, this force can be increased only by more love from one to the other. It has taken time, and numerous forms of mediation, to make man capable of hearing more and more the thundering voice of God. This voice did not make itself heard only through Christ; it made itself heard, in varying degrees, through Buddha, Plato, Socrates, Mohammed and other great incarnations of religious and moral genius that mark and foster the march of mankind. Christ is the greatest incarnation of all, since he is God Himself made man, in the sense that he embodies the greatest concentration of goodness and wisdom ever to manifest itself on earth. He sums up all that God had given men before his coming, and he illumines their road for the future. God is One man, but mankind is not one; it is multiple, and God respects this multiplicity which is the natural outcome of His activity in time, and He gives each aspect of mankind and each moment of time the appropriate amount of light that it can receive, and in the way it can make use of it according to the means possessed.

Life on the shores of the Mediterranean is not life on the banks of the Ganges or of the Yang-Tse; therefore, though Plato and Buddha have a good deal in common, each has his own distinct voice, which echoes his own background and the people who surround him. Christ, the confluence of many strands—Eastern, Western, Jewish, Greek, Egyptian and Indian—speaks with a voice which is his own, and which proclaims a truth that is nearest to God's truth, since it embraces the greatest synthesis so far of human efforts, attention and longings for God's voice and light. Buddha's voice is attuned to ways of living and thinking which are also part of God's creation, and therefore, in as far as they are informed with the spirituality that is God's essence, it expresses or mediates God's truth in ways which make it possible for this truth to be apprehended by those to whom it is destined. God always answers according to needs, and to the capacity one has to receive Him, and if St Francis and St John of the Cross are God's chosen vessels to teach wealthy, bustling Western man the virtues of poverty and stillness, Indian or Islamic people, who

61

already know poverty and practise stillness, as inherent in their lives, do not need to have them preached at them, and their Buddhas and Sufis can therefore concentrate, like their Western counterparts, on the love of God and the love of man. Gandhi, though not a Christian, is more truly Christian than most Christians, because he has, like so many extraordinary individuals—saints or sufis—the sense of the sacred which pervades creation, irrespective of time and place, and the urge to cooperate with God's will for the betterment of man. Such virtues are not a matter of churches, symbols or liturgies, but a question of divine inspiration, or rather of mediation of God's presence according to the community of men to which one belongs. The church only adopts these individuals once the impact of their actions has made itself felt, but not only does it not necessarily foster them, it very often opposes them, and even severely condemns them. Their true church is not the church, but the world, and the ills they seek to minister to are the sicknesses, suffering and death that afflict it. These ills are as inherent in man as the need to transmute them into the spirituality of the accepted cross is part of the necessary journey from God to God through creation and time.

Most men would be grateful for life even if there were no after-life, for the world of the senses unfolding in a universe fully harmonised by spirit is beautiful. Life can be lived at various levels, but it can be beautiful only when body and mind, matter and spirit are one, and are aware of being one in moments that transcend time. If the body is maimed, or if it is swamped by suffering, the spirit can be deadened, or even finally denied, and God with it, for there is no possible separation between body and spirit, and no salvation of the one without the other, or at the expense of the other. The body can never be reduced to being the accursed, sin-laden element of a manichean division of life into two parts. Life is one, and everything in it is informed with God's subsistent essence, and equally important in His vision which transcends churches and countries, and spreads to all things, in the same way as the rays of the sun embrace all things—the high and the low, those who are bright today and those who will only be bright tomorrow but are dark today, bearing in mind that tomorrow, in one way or another, always comes. St Francis loved all things, and St

John of the Cross loved night as well as day, because he knew that night would unfailingly give birth to day and light.

Creation is necessarily imperfect; it implies a withdrawal of God's burning light, so as to allow things to be what they are, according to the essence which is part of Him but which is not fully Him, since it does not have existence which can only be achieved through matter informed with His essence, unfolding according to its law, without constant interference or order from its source. This law is of course the law of love, the law of relating to a source which is love, through a natural appetition for it, and not through any outside compulsion. The appetition of the individuated essence for its source can come into play only if the individual can divest himself of all the impediments that prevent him from listening to it, and therefore from connecting with it. The same process enables the individual to get out of himself, to understand the other, to share in his suffering and, by so doing, to take up part of his burden. The experiencing of the other as a living subject can take place only through essence or pure subjectivity as imagination which makes it possible partly to take the place of the other, to become the other, and thus to recreate the other by communicating to him the essence that makes him and redeems him. This exchange between two subjects is an act of creation which can take place only through the mediation of the subsistent essence of life. In a similar way, sympathy, or suffering for the other, can take place only through the love of the essence of the Creator, Who is present in every creature, and therefore loves Himself through multiplicity. Truly to love the other is to love God Who loves through us. Eckhart says that God could not realise Himself without making His potential actual as Creator, namely by creating that which could respond to His love, by loving Him in return, and that God as love could not be satisfied without loving self-expression. Pure Being must cast shadows in order that it might see its own shape, and in order to know itself it has to differentiate itself into an infinite number of finite selves, each seeking to know itself both as different from and as part of the whole, and each seeking to forsake plurality for oneness.

Just as one can love truly only through the mediation of Being, one can know truly only through the mediation of

Being, so that both to love and to know are creative acts, the result of which is beauty and truth. Keats's equation of the one with the other was right; beauty cannot be dissociated from truth, and the love of beauty is a religious feeling which has played an important part in man's life since man differentiated himself from the animal. Even as a cave-dweller, man must have been awe-struck by the beauty of dawn, the sunset, a rainbow, a leaping river or the thousand moods of the sea. Beauty cannot be reduced to positivistic, mathematical measurements or logical assessments, it can be apprehended intuitively only as a metaphysical concept in which the apprehending subject knows and is aware of himself as being one with the apprehended object, in a creative moment which is its own finality. Such moments combine Apollo and Dionysus, and echo the moments of illumination of Christian, Buddhist or Islamic mystics. For the Greeks, beauty was a religion; equilibrium, harmony, perfection of lines, coherence, were its attributes, corresponding to the perfection of the Platonic Idea. The Bible, with the *Song of Songs*, the *Book of Job*, *Isaiah*, is one of the greatest records of the beautiful things of life, and of the beauty of God's world. Buddhism and Islam show practically, though in very different ways, as great a concern for beauty as Christianity, which, throughout the Middle Ages and up to the Renaissance, looked upon beauty as a homage to the Divine that holds the world in perfect harmony. The earth reflects the heavens. The song of birds, the beauty of nature praised by St Francis, the great cathedrals—Norman or Gothic—the statues, the countless paintings of Christ or of the saints, the carved scenes from the Bible, form a vast alphabet with which man spells his sense of beauty and his love of the Divine.

The loosening of the hold of religion upon the Western world, the growing dissatisfaction with it, did not affect man's love for beauty until the nineteenth century, when, religion being at its lowest ebb, beauty itself became the object of a cult to which many artists, dissatisfied with society and their time, paid tribute as the only value worth upholding. In spite of our contemporary scepticism and nihilism, this notion has not been finally uprooted from the heart of man, who no longer builds beautiful churches, paints beautiful pictures or carves beautiful statues, but whose search for the expression of his own individual truth, whatever the cost, has at times, about itself, an aura of absoluteness and transcendence that connects with the Divine. Though, in our materialistic world, nature is too often used as a means for utilitarian ends, men have not become fully robot-like, alienated from it. There is, in fact, an increasing love of rusticity, a longing for a return to a way of life that is lost, and for a sense of mystery and awe at the sight of mountains, forests or unchanging seas tossing on their waves the flotsam and jetsam of civilisations which haunt their dreams. The ideal world recedes; our world is in the grip of the senses as means of instant satisfaction; it cares neither for the past, for memories of yesterday, nor for the future, which is merely an embodiment of egotistical desires. Love of nature, love of the other, become in such cases love of self, without any mediation of the Divine, and therefore without any possible prolongation beyond the ashes that are the only outcome of such brief solipsistic fires. There is no room for the other. There is only the naked, anthropophagous self, feeding on other selves in a growing twilight in which the concept of man fades away into the falling dark where lies the discarded Nietzschean God.

Yet it is no doubt a mistake to equate Nietzsche's proclamation of the death of God with a total rejection of the Divine, while in fact he rejected only some aspects of it. This quotation from *The Gay Science* makes clear his attachment to metaphysical truth: 'The question "Why science?" leads back to the moral problem: "For what end any morality at all, if life, nature and history are not moral?" . . . But one will have gathered what I am driving at, namely that it always remains a *metaphysical faith* upon which our faith in science rests—that even we devotees of knowledge today, we godless ones and anti-metaphysicians still take *our* fire too from the flame which a faith thousands of years old has kindled: that Christian faith which was also Plato's faith, that God is truth, that truth is divine.' (*The Gay Science*, in *The Portable Nietzsche*, Viking Press, New York, 1954, p. 450) A contemporary of Nietzsche, Dostoyevsky, as great a genius as he was, and another, Baudelaire, though a lesser genius than both, were also obsessed with the sense of guilt and with the awareness of evil as non-being; they both strenuously opposed nihilism through their work, and for both Christ was still very much alive.

65

Nietzsche's superman is not the first man like Christ, he is the after man, he is what comes after the last man. He is not the logos who preaches humility and forgiveness, and who entered history to redeem man and to show him the way to God; he is man beyond man, more than man, who makes himself through his god-like will, willing itself as essence of being, and therefore recognising and accepting what necessarily is and can neither be rejected nor negated. This will, which is oneness and total positiveness, without negation or refusal of any aspects of being, obviously coincides with the will of Being, or the will of God, source and subsistence of life. Being or the value of values, for Nietzsche, can be reached only by the will to power, simultaneously aware of total nihilism, that is to say aware that absolutely nothing is worth anything, and that there is only the will seeking its true being as part of Being, which is the Eternal Return of the same.

Nietzsche's nihilism is at the opposite extreme of the everyday notion of nihilism which generally suggests negation of life, destructiveness and refusal of any positiveness. Nietzsche's nihilism is a total rejection of all the old values, and the creation of new ones, through will to power or will to being. It is both an end and a beginning, a journey through a dark tunnel where life was bogged down, and a return to a new, joyful life, unfettered by all the negative aspects of Christianity which Nietzsche saw as destructive and debasing of noble values. It is the snake eating its own tail, shedding its old skin and emerging in its total newness, free from all the impediments which say 'no' to life. Nietzschean nihilism precedes and prepares for total renewal as part of the Eternal Return of the same. The will to power is the will to being, not a negation of being, and the superman is the phoenix rising from the ashes of the last man, who had to die so as to be reborn and to proclaim a new religion, a new faith in life, in which appearance and reality are one, and in which, therefore, truth, in spite of its multiple appearances, is also one and immutable like God, to be discovered by the will to power as will to what truly is. The Nietzschean approach to truth is not very different, in its final outcome, from the Augustinian notion of truth as mediated by Being, or truth through the night of unknowing of the mystics. We are, in all cases, in the realm of necessity, in which truth and beauty are what they are, without any externally imposed finality, for finality implies conceptualism and interference with the true will or essence of creation.

Creation, issued from Being, is both beautiful and true in its totality, but the problem is to see or to grasp the totality, or, failing that, to be aware of the fact that every aspect of it is part of a whole, that therefore the sun, the seas, rivers, mountains can be both beautiful and terrifying according to circumstances. But they are absolutely objective and impartial, irrespective of human beings. Rains fall without discrimination on the parched deserts of Africa as well as on the swamp-covered, flood-ridden lands of Bengal. In one place, they bring beneficent growth and joy to men, in the other, they only add death and sorrows to a world already having its full measure of both. Our world is made up of such contrasts which are neither willed nor purposeful. The hand that rocks a baby to sleep pulls the trigger or drops the bomb that kills scores of them; the discovery that can relieve pain and save human life can destroy millions; birth and death are always side by side, sometimes in the same room, and the joy of the one is often withered away by the harsh wind of the other. Things are what they are, and they cannot be otherwise. Will and purpose are in man, not in them, and it is up to him to be able to see that the rains of Africa and those of India are both exactly the same, falling with equal indifference on those dying of thirst, who thus welcome them, and on those who are drowning in them, and thus curse them. They are part of the order of the universe, like Job's wealth, joys and sores, and unless man is able to reconcile both into the positiveness of life, he will spend a great deal of his time in perplexities, denials of life and barren sorrows.

The world and life are beautiful for those who are not overwhelmed by spiritual or economic burdens, and who can look at them in their truth; this does not mean any blind Leibnizean optimism, but the courage to accept, and therefore to master one's own destiny which entails sorrows, suffering and death; it means the acceptance with understanding and equanimity of the beneficent as well as of the searing rays of the sun, for the sun could no more take personal care of every individual on earth than God could take care of every personal desire, need or fear of men past, present and future. The sun is the sun—'midi le juste' of Nietzsche as well as of Valéry—immutably gazing upon space and time, and pouring forth without discrimination the essence of its being which is warmth and light. It is the same with Being or God, Who cannot be personalised or made responsible for whatever happens on earth, without turning Him into a puppet-master instead of the Creator of intelligent, conscience-endowed creatures. The seas cannot always be smooth, the winds cannot always be asleep in Proteus's cave. They have to be let out, it is a law of nature, and when they are out, they destroy all around them, uproot trees, overturn boats, and spread death on lands and seas. To ask why there are such winds makes no more sense than to ask why there is rain, why the sun. Man is given the mind to be aware of death, joy and sorrows, and he is given the inner light which, irrespective of shipwrecks and trials, will nevertheless lead him to his Ithaca, where undying love waits for his return; but he will find the journey long, arduous and barren if, when over the seas that unavoidably carry him to his appointed port, he spends his time cursing winds and waves, and has to be dragged unwillingly where he cannot avoid going. Odysseus knew that, in spite of Circe, Calypso, the Cyclops and other trials, he would in the end reach Ithaca. He is the hero guided by the gods to his destiny; we are all guided by ours, but we cannot all be heroes, and therefore we commonly refuse to face up to our destiny, or like grief-laden, immortal Calypso, we wish it were otherwise.

Man's problem is to know himself, and to know his destiny, and by knowing it, accept it and, in fact, make it. But the 'know thyself' of Socrates is merely a tag phrase, which strictly speaking is not applicable to man, who can never know himself. Only God can know Himself as God and contemplate Himself throughout eternity. Man cannot know himself in isolation. He can know himself only as part of a whole. To know oneself means to know what one is in society, creation and the universe, and in relation to Being. Knowledge of this kind is not biological or physiological knowledge, but knowledge of what man truly is, of where he comes from and where he goes, and what place he occupies in the universe. It is in fact metaphysical or religious knowledge, and it enables man to have an awareness of his true place and importance in creation. It is infinitesimally small, and whether he shouts or laughs, walks backwards or forwards towards his destiny, makes no difference whatsoever to the immutable order to which he belongs. A tiny insect caught in an irreversible flood, he can struggle as much as he likes, he can only go in the direction of the current. The moment man becomes aware that his breath cannot stop a hurricane, that his hand cannot smooth away the seas or the sorrows of mankind, and that burying his head in the sand does not save him from passing storms, he will cease being alienated from his surroundings and from life, and with greater or lesser eagerness, or at least with patience, he will say 'yes' to all aspects of life. He will say 'yes' to the joyful, and also to the sorrowful, for he knows that he cannot alter them in their essence, while, on the contrary, he can make of them practically what he chooses, according to his vision of life. If he looks upon life as a continuous feast of sensual pleasures and moral satisfactions, with God the Father providing him with all that he requires, then he is bound to come up against unbearable moments of suffering and sadness which will prompt him to inveigh against the absurdity and irrationality of the world. Yet the lurking shadow of death cannot be kept away by banquets, Mozartian music or Watteau-style fêtes. Neither can human suffering be assuaged or disposed of by Luciferan attitudes of opposition and negation.

Life is not negation, but positiveness; it is becoming, not non-being, it is acceptance, not refusal, and the only examples to live by are the saints and the tragic hero. Both live by the truth of Mary Stuart's motto: 'In my end is my beginning', and the end holds for both neither terror nor fear. They walk towards it, with steady steps, like men—not unwillingly, backwardly yet unavoidably, like crabs. For the saint and the tragic hero, everything that happens in life is necessary, therefore welcome, like flowers on a rough country road. There is no absurdity, no chance; all things, all events flow unavoidably from the beginning. If one is born with a clubfoot, and with the mark of fate or of genius on oneself, one will be Oedipus or Byron, and death will redeem both. Oedipus calmly went through the hoops that the Parcae had prepared for him, and after casting much light and causing many sorrows in the course of his earthly journey, he came to a numinous death in a sacred wood near Athens, which thereafter derived protection and strength from his shade. Byron's life was not ruled by the Parcae, but by his daemon which led him to die at Missolonghi, whence the light of his genius still breaks intermittently upon the world. For the saint and the tragic hero the end is always the beginning, and conflicting, disparate appearances fade away into the reality of the ineluctable order of things. 'In Thy will is our peace', said Dante, and the problem for man is to discover what this will is and to conform with it, for it is the indeflectible will that keeps creation in being.

Basically the world still is what it was in the days of Aeschylus and Sophocles, or in the days of St Francis of Assisi. Human life has been prolonged and greatly improved by science; men have gone to the moon, rockets have gone to Venus and Mars, but suffering and, above all, death still dance attendance on every human life. The quality of life has been greatly altered, the quantity of physical suffering may have diminished, but the quality of moral suffering has increased, and the quality of death has considerably deteriorated. Death has become stealthy and shameful, something one tries desperately to avoid, and once it has taken place, to disguise and forget as if it did not exist, or as if it could be transformed by embalmings and beauty treatments that try to hide its stark horror and its ineluctable finality. Yet man cannot know how to live unless he knows how to die, and to know how to die is something that cannot be rehearsed, for there is only one single and last performance, and the leading actor is no longer there when the curtain falls, so that he cannot hear the applause or the boos from the audience. He cannot know whether he acted well or badly; the way he acted depends entirely on the way he has prepared for the performance during his life. If, being truly aware of the tragic end of life, he began progressively to familiarise himself with this idea and to accept it as something unavoidable—which, to the believer or the materialist, is a vital moment, the most vital moment of life, either because it is a beginning or because it is an end—then he might make of it an end worthy of the life he has led.

The awareness of death entails the acceptance of the order of things, which man cannot change, except in the way he endures it and gives it meaning. In the light of this awareness, every aspect of life will be assessed by man in relation to his impending end, and he will live, not as if he were eternal, but as if every moment were to be his last. If he lived in such a way, it is very likely that, with the exception of the few who, by nature, are insensitive to others or to what surrounds them, he would be most careful not to hurt or cause suffering to those who share his plight, and whom he runs the risk of never seeing again, in which case he would never be able to undo the harm he had done. He would live his life in the noonday light of the sun, his consciousness ever holding within its grasp present and past, and always ready to be transformed at any moment into what he does not know but which will be his eternal sameness— the moment lived as absolute consciousness, transcending past and present and projecting itself into the future. Such moments are evidently rare; they are the mystical moments of the saint, or the inspirational moments of art; yet they can be approached and guessed at by all men, for if mysticism and true art are the privilege of the few, they can be emulated at all levels of life. Not everyone can be St John of the Cross, but every man can face up, every now and then, to his own night of unknowing, and draw from it enough light to make him aware of impending death, and therefore of the great joys and positiveness that life offers him, while he is still alive. In a similar way, if only the few have the courage to say: 'In my end is my beginning', and to maintain alive and constantly burning into their conscious-ness the single knot of light enfolding end and beginning, every man ought to make use of the great gift of life, not in order to squander it blindly or, least of all, to take it away from others, but to bring to himself and to others joys and love which will make the impending end, which he should never forget, all the more acceptable in that he will have totally fulfilled the span of life's possibilities allotted to him. In this manner he might be able to leave life with the detached stoicism of Seneca, the blessed illumination of St Francis, or the calm nobility of La Fontaine, whose wish was:

> Sortir de la vie ainsi que d'un banquet,
> Remerciant son hôte et faisant son paquet.

6

Atheism and Humanism

Atheism explicitly or implicitly posits the negation of the existence of God and the demystification of this notion, on the grounds that it is irrational and that it stems from a lack of lucidity, not to say bad faith, or a wilful or pathological urge to believe in it. This attitude assumes of course a pseudo-objectivity and a pseudo-scientific detachment which, in fact, do not exist. Whether one believes or refuses to believe, one can do so only out of conscious or subconscious convictions which one tries to rationalise; but to think that one can succeed in doing so is to take one's desires or evasions for logical realities. The passion to prove that God cannot possibly exist all too easily turns atheism into anti-theism, something which, somehow, in a vague way, presupposes the existence of something hateful and which must, at all cost, be negated. There is, in this kind of atheism, a substratum of Nietzschean nihilism or total negation of all values, in order to reconstruct a new way of life, that is to say a humanism, with men entirely free from what is described as the constricting presence of God. This kind of atheism looks upon faith as Angst, as a psychosomatic disorder which psychoanalysis or some other treatment could easily put right, or as a kind of biological failing which could be attended to by medicine or surgery. There is the superficial atheism of anti-clericalism, making use of all the past and present weaknesses of the Church and churchmen in order to conclude that faith is obscurantism and that religion is anti-human. There is Marxist atheism, that which looks upon religion as the opium of the people, and there is philosophical atheism which criticises faith and religion as mere animism, simplistic need for comfort, father-fixation, etc.—all weaknesses which a good dose of Comtean positivism could easily cure, thus liberating man from all these fears, with, at times, the help of Marx or Nietzsche. There is finally the type of atheism based on revolt, à la Camus, which expresses a serious ethical concern for the absence of God, but which totally ignores the illogical aspects of its own argumentation.

The attitude of revolt, contingent upon the notion of the absurdity of life, contradicts, in fact, the notion of the absurd. To revolt implies something to revolt against, some kind of authority or order, for to revolt against the absurd, of which one is necessarily part, is in itself absurd, sinks the whole matter into tautology, and is analogous to the paradox of the Cretan liar. Revolt can take place only against some kind of order, which one disapproves of, but which, of course, is not compatible with the notion of the total absurdity of life, that is to say with the notion of the absurd as an absolute. If one passes from the absurd as an absolute to the domain of the absurd as an attribute of life, that is to say to the domain of a certain order, or lack of order, one finds oneself in the domain of reason or lack of reason, which is antithetical to the notion of the absurd, and which is the domain of being and non-being, part of Being, which can be denied for all sorts of reasons, but none having any more validity than those used to prove its existence.

All in all, the anti-believing attitude oscillates between the anti-theism which allows God just enough existence for Him to be the butt of hatred, curses and spite, and the atheism which looks upon the idea of God as a figment of distressed, neurotic, irrational people who cannot face up to life or death, except with the drug or the prop of a God Who is purely of their own making. These people are looked upon with commiseration and condescension by those who see themselves as endowed with higher rational powers and a clarity of mind that saves them from falling victims to such calamities, and from being in need of such cheap comfort. But of course, believers in God are not all half-wits, psychopathic patients or weak-minded simpletons afraid of the dark and devoted to astrology, chiromancy, etc. They are at least as mentally well-equipped as those who despise their beliefs. Then the only explanation possible is that, though they may possess the brains and the facts which would make it possible for them to reach the same conclusions as the atheists, they are prevented from doing so by weaknesses and lack of will and courage to face the truth, which for them is pragmatic and experimental or, given the right axiom, an incontrovertible mathematical truth. Yet God is neither a perceptible fact nor a mathematical truth, and His presence in human life seems to be so necessary that some of the foremost atheists of the last hundred years, from Nietzsche to Sartre, have shown that the so-called death of God, and His absence, weigh more heavily upon their minds than twenty-five centuries of civilisation.

Nietzsche was a mystic and an outstanding religious and prophetic genius, deeply drawn towards the spiritual and the joyful creativity of life. Dionysus, for him, is joy and creativity, and Zarathustra seeks to rise as spirit towards spirit—the Supreme Divine, the value of values. Nietzsche's objections to faith are more ethical than religious; the God Whom he rejects is the God of heaviness and of the various denials of life, the God Who forbids joy and freedom, but not the God Who is the Being of beings, infinite source of becoming, Whose will to power aims at bringing about the eternal return of the perfect being. Nietzsche was brought up in the Christian faith, and his quarrels with certain aspects of Christianity are those of a deeply religious mind who never forgot the importance of 'the Crucified': 'The irony for those who think that Christianity has been superseded by modern sciences of Nature is that the value judgments of Christianity have not been superseded. "Christ on the Cross" remains the most sublime symbol, even now.' This was written in 1885 or 1886. (Nietzsche, *Gesammelte Werke*, Kröner Verlag, Leipzig, IV, p. 313) In 1881 he wrote to his master Peter Gast: 'You might find my ceaseless arguing strange and even painful, yet this is the best element of spiritual life that I have ever known . . . In the end, I am the descendant of a long line of Christian ecclesiastics . . . Forgive this narrowness.' (*Friedrich Nietzsches gesammelte Briefe*, Inselverlag, Leipzig, IV, p. 63) Eight years later, at the onset of his fatal illness, he sent a last note to his master: 'Sing for me a new song; the world is transfigured; the skies rejoice.' (Ibid., p. 437) Through Zarathustra the Superman, the anti-Christ, Nietzsche ceaselessly pursues his search for his anti-self—the creator of life and values, the eternal law-giver who will lift up life from the marshes of self-pity, lack of moral fibre and positiveness, onto the shining sphere of the Eternal Return, where the God-man or the man-God—the new Christ—lives and dies not on Calvary, but in the eternal light of Being.

Sartre, in *Le Diable et le Bon Dieu, Les Mots* and in some pages of *L'Etre et le Néant*, shows clearly that he cannot reconcile himself to the absence of God, that just as a child is despairingly anxious to discover his missing father, he misses the absent God, so that: 'We are compelled to realise that the real is an abortive attempt to achieve the dignity of being the cause of itself. Everything takes place as if the world, man and man in the world never succeeded in producing anything else but a failed God.' (*L'Etre et le Néant*, Gallimard, p. 717) The notion of God as Father is part of most religions, therefore it is normal that the notion of liberation from the Father should, with the rise of rationalism, be equated with the notion of man's liberation from God. One may be afflicted with the Freudian Oedipus complex, and wish to kill one's father, one may want to shake off his authority as a mark of adulthood, and this is an idea which from Nietzsche or Marx to Sartre has had a long run, but such an idea ill applies to God Who cannot be reduced to Jehovah or to thunder-wielding Zeus. Beside the notion of God the Father, there is Christ, the defender of prostitutes, of the poor, the rescuer of Lazarus from death, and the inspirer not of fatherly terror, but of brotherly love. However stern the Father may have been, few are the philosophers who have been able to dispose of His absence without the awareness that the world without Him is incomplete, for, as Sartre says: 'Everything takes place as if the in-itself and the for-itself were, in relation to an ideal synthesis, in a state of disintegration, not because such an ideal synthesis has ever existed, but precisely because it is always suggested, and always impossible.' (Ibid.) There is therefore the awareness of a lack, of something missing, and human consciousness can never get rid of the unhappiness caused by it. The image of God as a stern father, as a kind of Zeus, ignores Prometheus-Christ, the giver of pure love and hope. Therefore one can dispose of certain aspects of God, but not of God Himself, for God cannot be objectified or provided with predicates that can be condemned and rejected. God can be thought of only as a subject addressed by a subject, not in a posture of demand, but in the communion of prayer and elevation towards the beauty and harmony to which the subject aspires. The man-God relation can only be a relation of love, total love—mental and physical, that of a subject for a subject, as part of the intersubjectivity that underlies creation.

'If God does not exist, everything is possible', said Dostoyevsky in *The Brothers Karamazov*. This thought seems to be true in more than one way. Without a categorical imperative, inferring the presence of the supreme good, as Kant suggested, it is difficult to evolve principles of morality that could be valid for all men. If there are only secondary values, without a value of values as Nietzsche put it, or an ur-value, hypostatising itself as absolute, and therefore acting as the ultimate reference or golden mean for all values, these secondary values are all contingent and can in each case be negated by any one of them, when it cannot assert itself without excluding that which contradicts or stands in its way. This, in the final resort, can only lead to opportunism and to the destruction of any value that opposes one's appetites, desires or instincts. In brief, values without the notion of value itself as an absolute open the way to an anarchy of values, each having in turn its day or its moment of triumph, according to circumstances. But in the end, no value can be upheld against another, unless there exists a basic or central reference which could only be the supreme good, Being as fount of being, and not Being as a fixed object. Man is both existence and essence, but existence by itself would be purely contingent, deprived of the rationality and finality inherent in its source, which sustains life and is the foundation and final criterion of value as value.

Absolute death would be a denial of the value of the spirit that informs life and feeds its noblest aspirations in all domains —faith, science, art and action. From time immemorial, man has endeavoured to transcend time and to rise to a spiritual reality that defies change, since it is the fount and finality of creation. Such a reality is what Valéry described as 'midi le juste', the noonday sun or pure, objective light, mediating between man and man, man and God, and the multiple and the one, of which man has constantly dreamt from the birth of his consciousness, and which he faintly descries beyond the horizon, as one faintly guesses the coming dawn through the still grey haze of a winter morning. Without a categorical imperative, morality can only be relative and contingent upon individuals, societies and historical time. Then one has what Pascal saw—'truth on this side of the Pyrenees, error on the other side', and the truth of Cesare Borgia will never meet the truth of the fisherman or the peasant who has to work for his daily bread.

Relative morality is bound to be utilitarian, pragmatic and dependent upon circumstances. Reason is very unevenly distributed among men, therefore humanism can only provide variegated aspects of morality which cannot all be reconciled into universal principles. What is rational for one is not quite so for the other, for reason is never free from affectivity, and when it applies itself to behaviour and to moral decisions, it is never entirely free from the complex ethos of the person who uses it. Still, in spite of all these trammels on free judgments and on the objectivity of reason in the domain of ethics, it seems possible to achieve a wide degree of agreement about certain moral decisions, among people who possess more or less similar degrees of rationality and who have in common basic beliefs, attitudes and traditions. This, of course, only offers rather restricted possibilities for the application of purely rationalistic principles in the field of ethics. Leaving out the majority of people whose reason and conscience burn very dim at all times, and who are unable to evolve, through their own rationality, the rules and principles to balance their own impulses and instincts, and are therefore in desperate need of established criteria, to which, through belief and will, they could give allegiance for their moral life, there remains, for those who can reason, the important problem of finding means of discovering or elaborating the basic principles of morality to which they can all subscribe. The first and most important principle is, as previously stated, that life is sacred or holy. Yet how could one talk of holiness and sacredness to those who reject these notions in the name of rationalism? How could one explain, in a convincing and universalising way, that life should never be destroyed?

From the days of tribal life to those of religious and political fanaticism, to say nothing of our ideology-ridden world, there have been, and there are, countless instances of the application of the principle that the individual can easily be sacrificed for the good of the tribe, the faith or the party, etc. Communist as well as Fascist ideology attaches no importance to the life and well-being of the individual, who can easily be disposed of in the name of the good of the whole to which he belongs. Reason is the means by which one explains that, if the body has an abscess, this abscess must be removed for the good of the body. The falseness of the analogy between an individual body and the social body is easily glossed over in the heat of the ideological dogmatism that presides over such decisions. Reason cannot find the means to convince man, if man is looked upon as matter and nothing else, that it is never, or hardly ever, right to kill another man. The exception refers to acts of pure individual self-defence in the face of violent aggression and threat of death. This, of course, does not apply to cases of international aggression and wars, which are always the result of political preparations and corruptions, which involve, in varying degrees, the responsibility of all participants, and therefore could have been avoided, if the will to do so had truly been there. International wars are not instinctive acts to provide for or to defend life, as is the case in the animal world; they are calculated actions, often enough disguised under apparently noble motives.

Purely materialistic reason cannot make convincing the argument that a burglar caught in the act is never entitled to take the life of the jeweller or the policeman who tries to capture him. The burglar may be aware that he should not do so, and that these people are human beings like himself, with families, affections, hopes, dreams, etc., but the trouble is that these people stand in the way of his desires, his ambitions and his freedom, and, according to him, they ought not to do so. He will find all sorts of arguments to justify his actions; he will say that he has been unlucky, a constant victim of injustices, or that society—jewellers and all—is composed of crooks and robbers like himself, so why should he not apply some correctives to such corruption, and if jewellers or policemen intervene —well, it is bad luck; anyway, they are only the tools of a system with which he feels entitled to be at odds or at war. This does not mean that had he believed in God, in the categorical imperative of the sacredness of life, he would not have done that. Far from it. There are other complex questions which would need to be unravelled before one could decide whether or not such beliefs would effectively have prevented his action. They probably would, if some prerequisites were fulfilled, but for the moment let us briefly see if reason as the basic principle of humanism could provide the moral principle in the name of which individual life should always be respected, and suffering should never be inflicted upon others.

The only principle that could be used is the principle of utilitarianism basic to social life, which would not be possible if certain conventions and rules were not respected. If I can kill X or Y because he stands in my way, X or Y could do the same, so I'd better not encourage this type of behaviour. The same could be said about suffering, and that is good enough up to a point. But suppose that there are individuals who have enough power not to fear such reprisals, then there is nothing to hold them back. 'I must not kill a man because he is a man' is not reason enough, unless one is able to give the word 'man' a meaning that makes it clear that to kill a man is to kill an entity that cannot be reduced to a pure and simple aggregate of matter, since it carries within itself the breath which came to life with the first molecule, is laden with all the memories of man's millenary journey on earth, and is part of the energy or essence that brought life into being. This is what is holy or sacred, because it is something that cannot be replaced or remade, because to kill a man is to put out a living conscious- ness and to inflict a wound on the being to which we all belong. It is therefore to wound and to maim Being, and to be made to carry in our own conscience the dark shadow of ontological self-murder. Such feelings and visions can neither be explained nor summoned to life at will; they do not speak to man through reason; they speak to him and they come to him through the texture of his cells, which are more than chemical aggregates, and they emerge through his imagination which alone can keep present in his mind his birth as well as his death; with such a presence in his conscience, he cannot but respect life, which is indestructible and transcends the dominion of death.

Reason can tell neither what life is nor what death is; it can only describe them from the outside, as objects of observation, and not as experiences lived through a subject, and, while the knowledge provided by reason—knowledge of the laws of life and of the universe—gives man a certain power over both, it gives him none over their true being and finality. These can be apprehended only from the inside, not through observation but through consciousness. Suffering must be lived as part of one's life, and not viewed as something caused by something else; death must be lived as our own individual death, inherent in our life, and as its very purpose, inexorably intent upon its fulfilment, in the same way as the organic tends to revert to the inorganic. Death is what Mallarmé called 'ce peu profond ruisseau calomnié: la mort', and if it is so, one realises that, whether one is on one bank or on the other, one is part of a whole which no individual can attempt to wrench apart or wound without sacrilege, without hurting himself through hurting the other, for the other is also himself, part of creation, which is more than those who compose it, and more than individual reason can assess or define, though, of course, it can do a great deal to help man to move from the dark towards the light, from the fetters of ignorance towards the supreme freedom of knowing.

To be humane, to be a man, to behave as a man, are noble concepts, but they are very difficult to define, and above all, these concepts have evolved within a religious context which has fashioned them, and the predicates involved become, if they are deprived of their religious connotations, mere tautologies. Man as a body, without a soul, man deprived of his context of transcendence, is less than man, and cannot evolve a morality with claims to universality. Life deprived of spiritual dimensions is necessarily reduced to materialism, utilitarianism and hedonism, or search for pleasure. It is possible for Molière's Dom Juan to give a beggar a penny for the love of mankind, but what is mankind? The totality of human beings—all of them, black, white, yellow, rich, poor, good and bad? And how could I look upon them all as brothers, if we do not have the same Father, or if all of us on this earth are the outcome of a throw of dice, with a life-span which is nothing more than a breath and a gasp, both in one, and a death more absolute than rock? If everything stops at death, if our actions have no ontological import, and are confined to the purely social and historical plane, life will, on the whole, be devoted to the fulfilment of our satisfactions and ambitions on earth. No doubt, there are people whose ambitions are moderate, and whose desires are controlled by reason, which will not lead them to using others as objects, but such people, endowed with the necessary imagination to understand other people's problems, are few. Most men are dominated by forces and urges which make such serenity or Senecan nobility impossible, and their morality is likely to be a combination of indulgence to their impulses, and Machiavellianism to explain them. Good and evil, in such a materialistic world, are of no importance; what matters is success and power, and there is no moral sanction against these criteria of life as long as they do not violate social law. The state applies the same principle to the government of its citizens, and there is no moral redress against the criteria it uses, for the individual deprived of transcendence is a mere lump of organic matter, which can be treated as such for the fulfilment of the destiny of the whole to which it belongs and which controls it. No answer can be given to Stalin's order to kill a few million men, for what, according to him, was the good of the regime in power. These men were nothing more than bricks or stones to be used or discarded, in order to construct what he had in mind, and his mind was all in time, as pure immanence, making itself and making history in its own terms.

Without transcendence, it is not possible to establish the sacredness of the human person as belonging both to time and to eternity and contributing to the making of both. Time without eternity is merely mechanical, measured in terms of clocks, years and centuries, but without the continuum that gives it its dimension. Morality based purely on reason lacks models to follow, references to turn to in the final resort, and universalism to transcend societies, relative morality and historical moments. Reason can tell us to respect man, but cannot inspire us to love him, and respect for reason and logic cannot cope with individual passions and egoism, which can, if one accepts the axiom that self-interest is good, be built into a perfectly rational system. The problem with purely rationalistic ethics is always the axiom, the final reference one starts from or leads to, for from one form of good to another one is always compelled to come to some kind of good which is a moral obligation, a categorical imperative that cannot be transcended, and this only religion can provide. Intelligence and reason are vital to man, and without them no society or progress is possible; but man is something more than reason, he is a living organism, held together by mysterious and unexplainable forces, and it is to those who can strangely connect with the mystery of these forces that he owes the basis of the morality which has changed human life, because this morality transcends life and connects the rational with the irrational and with the obscure energy that causes life, and this energy is, on the physical plane, called love.

A purely humanistic ethic copes neither with man's natural egoism nor with political Machiavellianism, for without the sense of transcendence, man is not made aware of his innate weaknesses and urges to indulge his instincts, and he is deprived of the incentive to rise above them through love for his fellow beings and his Creator, for this love is only possible not as from one man to another—something which is always tinged with self-interest—but as love for the other through the truth and criterion of the source of love as pure giving, which is the love of God. This love is no guarantee against evil behaviour, cruelty and crime, for there have, in fact, been many crimes committed in its name, by people who used it in order to satisfy their own ambitions or misguided minds. Anyone fully aware of the reality of the love of God, of its implications in life and beyond life, could not perform an evil action. Evil is always a failure of awareness of the love of God and true goodness; it is a lack of knowledge, which might come later, but which is not part of the consciousness of the doer at the time when he performs his evil action. To possess such an awareness of the evil that one is about to perform, and therefore of the hurt it will cause to God or Being, and yet to perform it, is a daemonic act, which only a being temporarily controlled by forces or passions beyond his essential self could carry out. This does not mean that such a being is irresponsible, but it does mean that, as a human being, he was not, at the moment when he acted, in possession of the consciousness and the will which could have made it possible for him to conform with God's will. This will was, at that moment, negated and denied by desires and appetites which, had they been external to himself, would have made him irresponsible, but which were obviously part of himself, and which he was not able to control at the moment when they manifested themselves. Had he been in possession of normal mental faculties, he would have known that such behaviour was evil, yet, before evil manifested itself through him, he could not be clearly aware of its latency in himself, and of its disastrous import. Therefore he is partly responsible, for not having tried to analyse himself and to prepare himself against such possibilities, and partly not responsible, being unable to anticipate something which, up to that moment, was only virtual. The problem would be different with cases where there has been a steady progression towards evil; yet, whatever the pattern followed, the answer society must give to such behaviour certainly does not lie in the pure and simple suppression of the evil-doer, however tempting this solution may be. It lies, it seems to me, in finding appropriate and stern means of preventing the recurrence of similar deeds, and also of reforming the evil-doer and, if possible, giving him the chance to redeem his soul.

Man is only man as a manifestation of Being, and as an integral part of it, and not as an isolated, self-caused fragment in revolt against it, or unaware of his roots. The essential problem for man is the connection between thought and being. Man as a social being has an inherent urge towards the moral law, which he tends to associate with the rationality and reverence he attributes to natural laws, but the necessity for him to think or to become conscious of being is deeper still, since it is the necessity to think his essence. This necessity is ontological; it grounds ethics upon the reality of being; it transcends rationalism, logic or humanism, and it posits transcendence, not as the supreme value to be used as an objective golden mean of ethics, but as being which is both the source and finality of life, which makes itself as freedom issued from freedom and returning to it as absolute knowledge. Man is freedom, but can neither make this freedom himself nor provide himself with it, whatever means he may use. He is created as freedom, but he is not coeval with it; freedom overlaps him at his birth and at his death, and he can coincide with it only as part of Being which subsumes both existence and nothingness. Man is both incomplete, and, by himself, beyond completion, ever open to tomorrow, which he can reach only through ineluctable death. Tomorrow is always there, known for the One Who knows all, yet unknown to man who, though he can have an awareness of being, in time, can never know total being, not even when he is reunited with Being, for he has by then become knowledge, for self-knowing Being, through which he knows what he himself is, but not what Being is. Man is only man through his relationship with transcendence feeding his freedom, which is only perfect when the former coincides with it, and confers transparency upon his earthly finitude. Through this relationship, man sees himself in time, and beyond time, tied to the earth by his finitude, his materiality and his instincts, haunted beyond the earth and matter by visions of eternity, through love, faith, art and all the fire-fed aspects of life, which illumine his progress throughout the ages and give him the courage to be both himself and more than himself—the son of his Father, to Whom he unfailingly returns.

7

Religion

All religions are approaches to the Divine. Buddhism is described as 'the noble eight-fold path'; Confucius's message is called 'the way'; Shintoism is also a way, and Marxist praxis, for Marxism is a religion, the way to a New Jerusalem. All religions express and define the relationship between man and the ideal or the supernatural world, whether it is pure and simple animism which places the Divine in the sun, the seas, mountains, rivers or rain, polytheism or monotheism. In all religions the Divine requires to be mediated through things, natural phenomena or incarnations, and the finite human being can never come face to face with it, without losing his individuality and disappearing either temporarily or permanently into the Infinite. Neither the mystic nor Moses can confront the dazzling face of the Eternal; the Divine is always on the other side of being; it cannot be thought of, it can only be lived. God and man are not commensurate; they cannot communicate directly, as does one man with another. Their communication has to be mediated by forms, images or avatars which partake of both. A man cannot speak to a beetle or to a worm, and God can speak to man only in terms he can apprehend. That means that the Eternal can be apprehended only through a finite mind, which, therefore, makes it what it thinks it is, or what it reveals itself to be, which comes to the same thing, for both apprehension and receptivity are conditioned by the capacities of the human mind. But unless there were an appetition for God, and an inherent link between the two, there would be no search for or apprehension of the Divine. There is something in man that impels him to look for and to connect with being as part of Being, and whatever name one may give to this something, the mystery remains unsolved.

All human actions and behaviour imply conscious or subconscious urges, desires and compulsions which motivate them. Like everything else in life, they have causes, which one may or may not be able to analyse, but which fully justify the old dictum: 'ex nihilo nihil'. Scientific research rests upon the urge, the drive, whatever one likes, to uncover the laws of the universe. The religious or metaphysical quest rests upon desires, impulses or urges to understand the universe and life not in terms of pragmatic, experimental knowledge, but in terms of experience which satisfies the natural rationality of man. The aspirations of human reason towards the apprehension of the absolute merely express the true finality of spirit, and of man as a spiritual being. This search for the absolute through rational processes is no more nullified by the subjectivity of the impulses which motivate it, than the objectivity of scientific research, of philosophy or of the work of art is nullified by the subjectivity of the scientist, the philosopher or the creative artist. The main point when considering such matters is always to bear in mind Kant's warning to 'take great care that the principles that govern experimental knowledge may not transgress their boundaries and mingle with the principles of intelligible knowledge'. Religion and metaphysics belong to the intelligible world, therefore they cannot be approached, and least of all judged, in terms of concepts drawn from the experimental world, in which the predicate is not part of the subject, whereas in the intelligible world the predicate is always part of the subject as the basis of knowledge.

In life, the organic tends towards the inorganic which is death, that is to say towards its breaking up into atoms and molecules which will form new organic entities, and so on and so on, in an endless cycle in which matter and energy take different shapes according to their laws which leave nothing to chance. The pulsion towards death is part of life, and all the linguistic acrobatics and attempts to make of death something that is not inherent in man are useless. Expressions such as 'He died of this or that' cannot disguise the fact that he merely ran short of life, because death was in himself, and therefore was bound, at one moment or another, to have its say. Freud, who described religion as an illusion or a flight from the angst of life, was himself obsessed by death, an obsession that lies at the root of man's psychosomatic neurosis, and probably underlies a desperate longing for God, for a Father, or at any rate for a reassuring presence on the threshold of the dark. Yet religion is neither an illusion nor a compensatory projection or wish-fulfilment, nor a means of consolation and redress for the injustices and sorrows of earthly life. These are mere tauto-logical explanations for a fundamental fact which is as old as man's proto-history and history, and which is that religion is inherent in him; it is part of his essence, and therefore it could very well be looked upon as being what Plato thought it was—a memory of the Great One, or a dim awareness of Being, apprehended by individuated essence, issued from it and returning to it. Whatever the explanation one may try to use in order to dispose of religion, so as to make of it a purely anthropological notion born from man's limitations and incapacity to know the truth, it still leaves unexplained the fact that man, irrespective of the climes under which he lives and the time when he lives, always shows, by and large, the same constant basic longing for the supernatural, for something which transcends him and which is the Divine.

If man were a pure and simple aggregate of chemical cells holding together, as an organic entity, for a certain number of years, and then falling apart and regaining their place in the great whirling wheel of purely material life, these cells or the organism which they temporarily compose should have no awareness of, or longing for, something that goes beyond matter. But this is not the case, for, although we might be able to describe what exactly life is, in purely biological terms, we cannot say what life truly is, why there is life, whence it comes and where it goes. To know that proteins and enzymes form the living cell does not tell us how, from the amoeba, we have reached the wonderful combination of neurons that form the brain, the most extraordinary achievement of life, the kind of computer which can neither be unravelled nor repeated by human hands. We certainly know a lot about it but we do not know how or why, for millennia, it has been able to project itself out of itself into the world of ideas and the world of supernature, a world which defies physical laws and cannot be mapped out according to them. Whether these neuronic manifestations are due to the fear of death, to the urge to compensate for some unsatisfied longing, or to whatever one likes, these fears and desires are present in man, but they are not so in the animal; therefore, whatever the name one may give to man's longing for a world beyond himself, this longing is part of his consciousness; it is what is called religion, and is what is assuaged by religion.

It is true that animals have a kind of premonition of coming death, but man is the only animal who does not wait for impending death to have premonitions of it; he is aware of it from the moment he is able to think; he lives with it all his life, and the consciousness of it and the way he assesses it determine the way he lives and dies, and make something far more real than the ideologies and theories against which he may bruise his body and his mind. Consciousness of self is above all consciousness of being-for-death; it not only precedes consciousness for others and consciousness for history, but it underlies them and determines what we make them; this consciousness is both individual and multiple, and it unites all men in the intersubjectivity of being-for-death, which is an unavoidable, impending reality. What eludes, and has constantly eluded man, is the ground from which he passes from this reality to another, which, though not verifiable, is just as perennial and deep-rooted, and which is that death is turned into a beginning, an opening upon a world in which every one of the things of our world has been sieved and transformed into its lasting truth, a world, therefore, which is by essence beautiful and eternally true. Whatever scientific discoveries man may make, and the possibilities are as large as himself as a finite being, he will never succeed in explaining himself, that is to say in finding out what truly makes life or being, for that would mean life understanding itself and making itself, not as separate lumps of cellular tissues made in laboratories, but as individuated, organic entities with brains and all. This, if it ever happened, would mean that life had reached the stage of causing and sustaining itself, that is to say the stage of merging with Being. The cycle would thus be closed, and there would be only Being contemplating and knowing itself eternally, without any mediation through matter and time.

Religion is universal in its basic purpose, which is man's

relationship with the supernatural, and it also varies according to time and place; it takes various forms, and it displays varying rituals, though there exist a large number of common practices and a stock of myths and legends which are practically universal. The myth of the incarnation, that of the virgin birth, and that of water and fire, are some of them. Water and fire are always means of transformation, regeneration and rebirth. St John the Baptist baptised with water, Christ with fire; rebirth always takes place through water or fire. The soul passes through water, to the isles of the Blest, or through the Styx, or through fire in order to reach the state of bliss of Heaven or of the Elysian Fields. Fire is masculine, water is feminine, and both are necessary for birth and rebirth. That is why religions are not truly self-exclusive, but evolutionary, at times complementary, and in many ways all related in their approach to the Divine. That is why one cannot conceive of one single religion as being the chosen one, or the one and only valid approach to the Divine. Such a notion could only lead, as it has done in the past, to arrogance and fanaticism. First and foremost, all men, irrespective of time and place, are necessarily God's children, or individuations of being. It would be unthinkable to look, for instance, upon the pre-Christian era as a forsaken period, in which a whole mass of mankind was alienated from God because the Incarnation had not yet taken place, and to consider that this mass of souls, if soul there is, should be confined for eternity to a limbo world caught between being and non-being, because God decided to take on manhood only two thousand years ago. This would be as arbitrary and unworthy of an omnipotent and omniscient God as the notion that, since Christ was born in the Western world, this world is closer to God than the Eastern, or the world of Mayan civilisation or of Africa. God is God for all men, those who were born before Christ as well as those who live outside Christianity.

One might be led to think that Christianity embraces a greater number of qualities which, if put into practice, come closer to Divine perfection than either Buddhism or Islam, though this is partly a question of opinion and partly a question of the kind of criteria one applies in order to establish this scale of values leading up to supreme value or the Divine. There is, to my mind, no doubt that Buddhist tolerance and lack of proselytism are superior to the Christian urgency towards the propagation of the faith, and even more to Islamic imposition of faith by force of arms. On the other hand, the Buddhist negative attitude to life, and its flight from it, which, for a while, affected Christianity and Christian mysticism in the Middle Ages, amount to a refusal of being, to a rejection of its positiveness and of the fulfilment of all its possibilities in its individuations, and in history and time. The same could be said about the notion of suffering, which is crucial to both Buddhism and Christianity. For Buddhism, suffering must be avoided; this entails the annihilation of desires, and of the importance of the body which is looked upon as a hindrance to spirituality and bliss, and it entails also a rejection of matter as a source of suffering and as an impediment to spirituality. The outcome of these views is a total disregard for life in time, looked upon as maya or illusion, to be lived as a transition towards the complete refinement of the spirit, through as many incarnations as necessary, until it reaches the perfection which precludes its return to earth. For Christianity, suffering is a basic element of life, and its transcendence is both a means of knowledge and of coming nearer to the Divine. But there is, of course, a very great difference between the Buddhist annihilation of the self and Christian suppression of self-centredness and egoism as a prerequisite for the love of the other as well as for the love of the Divine.

All religions, whether they have grown side by side, or developed diachronically in time, interpenetrate one another and share common features. Many Christian churches rest upon the remains of pagan churches, and they even have, in some cases, incorporated fragments of them. David danced in front of the sacred ark, and dances by holy objects or fires are part of the ritual of most religions; so is fire itself. It is not for nothing that Prometheus stole it from Zeus, to give it to man as a gift which engendered greater power than the eating of the apple that Eve gave to Adam; although both gestures had the same outcome—chains on a Caucasian rock, with vultures ceaselessly eating the ever-born liver of the fallen Titan, and the whole progeny of Adam condemned to carry in suffering and sorrow the weight of original sin. Of course, Io, the daughter of Jove, came in the end to free Prometheus, in the same way as Christ, the Son of God, is said to have come to free man from the chains of original sin. Still, neither of these two operations could be said to be in any way creditable either to Zeus or to God Himself; so the least said the better, though it should be said that the notion of propitiatory and expiatory victims—lambs or even human beings—is part of practically all religions. So is the notion of the immolation of a bull, a youth or a god in order to bring about new life, new crops, favourable winds or the return of the sun to the hemisphere it has left. All these various accretions have no doubt coalesced around the figure of Christ as Saviour and Redeemer. Still, we have now reached the stage when the sacrifice of human beings, or of God, in order to redeem the failures of a people or of mankind itself, is no longer acceptable. This is all the more so in that the original fault for which a sacrificial victim has to be offered must always necessarily be traced back to some failings of the Father, and to the society that He created, and one cannot accept the idea of a father doing away with his own misdeeds by sacrificing one of his children, or his own incarnated self, if he is God, in order to make amends and to redeem the outcome of his own heredity.

Christ's sacrifice can be accepted only as an image of human life, as a ritual which implies a full knowledge and awareness of the error or evil committed by man, and as a true desire, in the face of God, to make amends for it and never to do it again. In this respect, the Holy Communion has its full meaning as an individual and a universal awareness of one's own responsibility to oneself, to one's own fellow beings and to God, Who sent Christ to mankind not to cleanse it with his blood, but to teach it how to face up to suffering and death in obedience to the laws of nature which are also the laws of God. Man communes with God through Christ—the mediator and Incarnation of the Divine; but an evolved mankind, as it is now, cannot look upon Christ as an expiatory victim whose death redeems its failings. Christ is the better image of man, the aspiration to the good, to universal love, to self-sacrifice for the other, not because the other is part of a sin-laden multitude, but because the other is like himself, in as far as he is a man, afflicted with sorrows, with, at times, unbearable suffering, and even more unbearable death; Christ shows his fellow beings—men—that all this must be accepted because it is part of God's will, that is to say part of the law of Being, and that this law, whether one smiles or cries, must be obeyed, for it cannot be altered, except in the way one accepts it. Our freedom does not consist in altering this law, but in what we make of it. This is, admittedly, not much, yet it is a great deal, for if the antelope crushed to death by a lion feels its life ebbing away without knowing why, man, when confronted with the tearing apart of his cells, knows that if he can manage to keep his faith in himself and in his Maker, and his dignity in this last and most terrible moment, he will have triumphed over death, for death will have the better of his body, but not of his mind, which is the apex of nature, and the magic mirror of the cosmos and of life itself.

Comparative study of religions has shown numerous similarities and mutual borrowings. Passing from Sumer to Egypt, Crete, India, Greece, Palestine, Rome and Mecca, one finds endless similarities in ritual, imagery, organisation and dogma; they show that the human mind is possessed of certain basic structures which make it possible for it to apprehend or to connect with the structures of the universe and of life, and to express such apprehensions in terms which bear the hallmark of the time and place when they were coined, but which basically convey the same unchanging truth. This is the true meaning of myths and archetypes which are part of man's memory or subconscious, and which are the basis of his perennial knowledge. The Shintoist heaven and the Valhalla of Nordic mythology are not very different; neither are Buddhist Nirvana and Christian Heaven. Nirvana means 'waning out', waning out of the suffering of life, identification of the individual self or *atman* with the universal self or *Brahma*, in a world which is neither existence nor non-existence. This world is admirably described in the words of Plotinus: 'It is unspeakable, for if you say something of it, you make it a particular thing', words which are echoed down the centuries by those of Master Eckart and other mystics, while the Buddhist denial of the self corresponds to Franciscan otherworldliness and other virtues that are as much Hindu virtues as they are Christian. Roman stoicism, expressed by Seneca, taught the followers of Christ, those who died in arenas as well as in the

94

solitude of prisons, that: 'God has a fatherly mind towards good men and loves them strongly, and He asks that they may be harrassed with pain and losses so that they may gain true strength.' This is not Job speaking, but Seneca who, strangely enough, said well before Leibniz: 'God made the world because He is good, and as the good never grudges anything good, He therefore made everything the best possible.' The type of stoicism, source of courage and will, that led Seneca to walk as calmly out of life as a Japanese samurai, needed to be tempered by the stoicism of Socrates and of the Greeks, who possessed a sense of the numinous and a spirituality which were totally deficient in Rome. The most moving event of Roman history is that which marks its beginning—the death of Queen Dido on her pyre on her Carthaginian shore, while Rome's founder, Aeneas, was leaving her to face alone the tragedy of her unrequited love. A thousand years later, Aeneas's descendants returned to these same shores, and they covered them with greater fires, and with salt, so that Dido's heirs should forever be cast into the dark. Thus it was that Dido's spirit never crossed the Mediterranean and never reached Rome; it returned to greater Greece, whence it had come.

Only the kind of fanaticism which has been the curse of the Inquisition and the Counter-Reformation can lead people to think that one religion is the chosen religion, the only way to God, thus condemning all the others as errors or heresies to be wiped out by force. Such an attitude would mean that at all times only a small fraction of mankind could really be part of God's concern; the rest would be either wilfully allowed to live as dross, or as corruption to be ignored, or destroyed as part of a manichean world, in which God had His reserved field of action while the rest was part of Satan's dominion. Such notions are, if not totally dead—*vide* the example of Catholic-Protestant or Christian-Moslem hatred, and the passion still displayed by some narrow-minded sects to convert everyone to their method of salvation—at least dying out and of less and less importance in a world more and more aware that we shall either be saved together or perish together. Eastern thought and Eastern religious attitudes are finding greater and greater support in the West, and it must be said that this kind of recognition of the need for fecundation of one religion or one civilisation by another, so as to produce blends of what is best in both, is beneficial to man. There is no doubt that Buddhism and Christianity have great similarities, and this is not surprising, for the Platonic and neo-Platonic elements that constitute an important part of Christianity are also part of Hindu thought which was in constant relationship with Greek thought during the pre-Christian era.

The human mind is one in its wholeness, and it throws forth thoughts and ideas which are its apprehensions of ever-changing reality, through different images, linguistic structures and symbols, but which are basically the same, irrespective of their phenomenal appearances. The thoughts and ideas that came to light through human brains in the sixth and fifth centuries BC, on the banks of the Ganges, on the Euphrates, or on the shores of the Pyreus, were at times very similar, and they did not need to be taken from one place to another by trading caravans or soldiers. The world of spirit knows no bounds; thought is synchronic; it is always present as the noosphere which images and reveals the laws of the biosphere; it emerges as part of human consciousness at many places at the same time, and if, in some places, a thought or idea is not recognised at once for what it is, it is because men are not ready to receive it, and therefore these will have to die, and new generations will be born, who will be attuned with this thought and recognise it as part of themselves and of their time.

If Christ is the incarnation of God, every Bodhisattva is an incarnation of the spirit of Buddha. Both Christ and Buddha forbade killing, and the pacifism of Gandhi is as Buddhist as it is Christian—or would be, if only Christ's doctrine had been constantly respected throughout the centuries; in fact, it has not been, and, worse still, even in our times there are priests and prelates who talk of holy wars and who bless soldiers engaged in colonial wars. Buddhism forbids the killing of animals, and commands respect for them, with an urgency that only St Francis advocated. Christ recommended the example of the lilies of the field, which neither sow nor reap; he chased the money-lenders from the temple, because wealth has nothing to do with happiness or faith; he told the rich young man to leave his wealth and to follow him; he loved Martha,

96

but he loved Mary more, because she could listen, and he gave more to the one who had worked less than the other, and thus needed more. Buddha left the wealth and comfort of the towns for a wandering life of poverty. Christ forgave Mary Magdalene and the sin of harlotry; Buddhism chastises the flesh and preaches the avoidance of lust and carnal relations, so there is no need of harlots. Buddhism emerged as the living expression of a society which naturally welcomed it, and seemed to be attuned to it. In that society, social stratifications and what is called elitism were accepted as unimportant, since what mattered most was not to stay in it, and to make one's way upward in it, but to get out of it, out of time, beyond the wheel of life, beyond the importance of the self and the individual, so dear to the West.

Roman civilisation in its stage of decadence was the manure that fostered and fed Christianity, which adopted its socio-political structures and infused them with a spirituality of which they were very much in need and which they had, at that time, completely lost. These socio-political structures were not the best acquisition of Christianity, for they gave it a legalistic and hierarchic framework which was not attuned to its spirituality, and which considerably hampered its true development. Christianity was originally the religion of a displaced and partly alien proletariat and of slaves, to whom Roman gods and goddesses had nothing to offer. Their aristocratic power games and intrigues among themselves, involving considerable sacrifices in the interests of achieving their aims or maintaining their power, had nothing to offer those who owned nothing, not even their lives. The Romans themselves had lost the will to power; they were merely upholding its trappings without any means or desire to defend them; they were concerned only with materialistic and hedonistic satisfactions, in a world without tomorrows. Christianity brought light to this grey, twilight world, yet it could not have done so unless darkness had already fallen; civilisations only die once they have lost their inner spirituality, and the Greek, the Roman and the Mayan were in as advanced a state of decomposition as Oscar Wilde's portrait of Dorian Gray when they fell an easy prey to their respective conquerors.

Christianity was born among people who were on the whole

constantly in conflict with the society in which they were living. It was above all a religion of survival, of projection towards the future, out of an intolerable present. As such, it was a religion of opposition to the existing parochial religions which embodied the beliefs and aspirations of the dominant people who oppressed and sought to destroy its followers. It was therefore an expansionist and proselytising religion, anti-social by nature and in some ways anti-life, since the life it was compelled to live as an underground struggle was essentially reduced to its spiritual aspects, and to a denial of the body which was, all too often, an instrument of suffering, toil, tortures and death, transcended only by the indestructible and perennial spirit. All indulgences towards the material aspects of life, such as sex, love of good food, comfort or luxury, were sinful, since they weakened the resistance of the spirit to social oppression. In such conditions, it is easy to understand why apocalyptism and projection into an other-worldly future were widespread. The end of the world was ever supposed to be at hand, simply because the world was unbearable. In fact, it was practically as unbearable for the slave as for the masters who had lost the will to live and the will to defend their crumbling faith and their way of life against the barbarian forces knocking at the gates. The descendants of the soldiers who had marched from Zama to the Danube, and from Greece and Egypt to Scotland were tired; they had lost faith in themselves, in their Empire, their laws and their way of life, which they had sought to impose upon the world. By now, whether at home or abroad, they did as little work as possible; they left it to their slaves to do their manual work, and to their mercenaries to fight for their frontiers and their safety, until in the end the mercenaries became their masters and fathers of their emperors.

Christian rejection of all the weaknesses of the body stood as an example that progressively imposed itself on a society which, having lost its nerve, saw in this a means of restoring it and shaking itself out of falling darkness. Having loved the world and the things of the world to the point of being corrupted and destroyed by them, these people, from now on, rejected the world in favour of a form of asceticism, monasticism and lack of concern for material well-being such as is inherent in Buddhism, and which in the West lasted until the progressive growth of Thomistic realism from the thirteenth century onwards. From then on, life in time became more and more important, good works, good actions became as important as faith, and social success was no longer looked upon as a betrayal of the spirit and a surrender to the satisfactions of the senses and of the ego, but as a means of doing justice to God's gifts and God's grace. Needless to say, from this attitude men moved all too readily towards attitudes that made it easy to reconcile their natural greed and appetites with the name of a good Christian, obtained through participation in good works and church attendance on Sundays.

Whether in Christianity, Buddhism or Islam, suffering is part of life. Allah's will is inscrutable, one can only say: Inch Allah, and take what comes. For Buddhism, suffering is the result of a wrong attitude to life, to be corrected through meditation and observance of the rules in order to achieve wisdom. For Christianity su ̃ering has always been part of life, and it has generally been looked upon as a means of exalting human virtues and rising toward the Divine. Yet it would be unwise to jump to the conclusion that all suffering is necessarily holy. Far from it. Suffering can also be abject and masochistic, if it is used for a given purpose, as in the case of the beggar or, worse still, the fake beggar, who exhibits his scars or deformities in order to attract pity and money. It is the same for any kind of weakness, if it is willed or used as a means to prey upon others, or to exercise power through displays of sorrows which obviously seek to elicit help. The true Christian attitude towards suffering is best expressed by the Cross as the symbol of human life. Christ expresses the true nature of human reality; all relations between God and man pass through him, through his actions and his words, and man can find peace and harmony with himself only by emulating the wisdom and courage of the one who came to earth to implement the Miltonic notion of justifying the ways of God to man, that is to say to teach him how to live and how to die. Every man must die his own death and work out his own redemption or refinement of spirit, through his own life and death, not through the death of Christ, but with the image and example of Christ as a guiding light.

It seems to me that, if to die in order to save someone who is in mortal danger can be a noble and altruistic action the noblest man can perform, to die in order to save someone from his own weaknesses, failings or even crimes is unwholesome for the one who does it, since it could be pure masochism, and for the one it is destined to save, since it reveals in him cowardice and a total shirking of his own responsibilities. Such attitudes would certainly be a very poor foundation for morality, which should rest on the clear awareness of what moral duty is and what a man must do in order to cleanse his conscience from the burden of his failings and errors. Whatever he does, he must certainly not ask somebody else to suffer or to die in order to bring him peace of mind and spiritual salvation. Christ on earth died because of man's stupidity and cruelty, and because he challenged a world order of established privileges, master-slave relations and materialism, which could not go down without reacting violently, but to look upon his death as having been willed from eternity, because of some so-called original sin or fault of mankind, is another problem which has constantly baffled human rationality and which, therefore, ought to be, once and for all, set aside. For what can one mean by original sin—carnal knowledge, or pure and simple search for knowledge, such as, for instance, scientific knowledge? God-made Adam was love-laden and intent upon procreation, therefore what else could he do but love and make love to Eve, his only companion, and procreate with her? As for the search for knowledge, that is a far more serious problem, for, if man were to be from the beginning forbidden to search for knowledge, and only allowed to know what God wanted him to know— something we are told nothing about—there would have been no progress whatsoever, and man would still be living under trees and in caves.

Whatever this forbidden knowledge was supposed to be, it certainly was not something whose discovery made man God-like, and turned him into 'one of us', as Genesis says. Man is destined to remain man, whatever happens; his knowledge will always be human knowledge, that is to say limited knowledge, and never God's knowledge. Therefore why should he not be entitled to human knowledge, which is strictly inherent in his prerogatives as man? God could not possibly begin life, the life of creation, with a purposeless 'don't', for everyone knows that 'don'ts' can only be made to be respected by brute force, supernatural fears, or by supplying a totally rational explanation for them. But it would be both irrational and ungodly to forbid man to think, that is to say to use his God-given reason, the thing that makes man what he is, for he is truly man only through thought and morality and through searching, as God Himself does, for greater and greater knowledge and freedom. Faith is all-important, but it would be very difficult to accept a faith that forbade knowledge, or certain forms of knowledge, for to know is God's very purpose through creation which is a progression towards His absolute self-knowledge. Sin could only be knowledge of the individuated self as separate from the universal self or God Who can know Himself only through the differentiations and negations of finite selves, and as such sin is part of God's necessity. Although the mistake has all too often been made in the past, reason and faith cannot be opposed. They are part of the whole man, and faith cannot be used to obnubilate reason without making of man something less than man, and thus making of his Maker something less than God. The obscurantism of some misguided prelates of the past who opposed scientific knowledge as a danger to the faith was a disaster for the faith which it discredited. But though such examples of obscurantism are all too easily multiplied and magnified by opponents of religion, they were and they are very few. Faith did not prevent Roger Bacon or Locke from believing in the value of experimentalism, Newton and Einstein from searching for the physical laws which are the structures of the universe, or Kant from exploring the range of reason. It did not prevent Thomas Aquinas, Suger, Abelard and many other famed medieval monks from upholding the point of view that there is no conflict between faith and reason.

Faith is of vital importance to man, but the Pauline cry of justification by faith has long since ceased to have currency, owing to the steady growth of reason and the unfolding of the dream of learning. Pascal's saying: 'I believe only in ideas men are prepared to die for' can no longer be accepted as a categorical imperative of the truth of ideas, in a world increasingly stained with fanaticism. The various terrorist groups and guerrillas of all kinds who claim to be motivated by so-called ideals of justice when they ruthlessly kill innocent people,

101

including children, cannot be looked upon as good men, or men of truth. Blood justifies nothing, and cannot be used as a test of truth. 'Blood', said Nietzsche, 'is the worst witness of truth; blood poisons even the purest doctrine and turns it into delusion and hatred of the heart. And if a man goes through fire for his doctrine—what does that prove? Verily, it is more of your doctrine coming out of your own fire.' (*Thus Spake Zarathustra*, in *The Portable Nietzsche*, Viking Press, New York, 1954, Part II, p. 205) Blood and violence prove nothing except the existence of violent natures or desperate situations, in which a man may have to kill in order not to be killed; but the point is that no morality can be built on blood, either as a redeeming or a justifying element. Justice does not proceed by blood, it goes through redress of wrongs done, and purification of soul, so that repetition of similar deeds may not take place.

Actions must be judged as actions, that is to say according to their import, and, on the whole, they are more important than the motivations or intentions they may be credited with, for after all, it is all too easy to say what one likes about them; that is part of the domain of imagination, but actions are events in time and with extensions in space, and they have causes and effects, which can perhaps be explained away, but not rubbed out. No casuistry can replace the import of action, and turn for instance murder into a noble deed, or revive the victim of this murder. The dissociation of faith from action leads to the dissociation of body from spirit, while they are one, and they cannot be treated as separate entities. We know the universe through our bodies, as well as through our minds, and every human action involves body and soul, except for the few mindless, soulless people who are more in need of sympathy and treatment than obloquy and retributive punishment. The body cannot be put through all sorts of actions which supposedly leave the spirit or the soul perfectly unaffected. Those who have been in concentration camps, in psychiatric asylums, know better, for they know how hard is the return to a spiritual sanity and equilibrium which has been practically destroyed by physical as well as by mental tortures. The body has its reasons, which reason cannot rationalise, but the two cannot be separated as belonging to different categories of life, for it is their oneness that makes life on earth and beyond what it is.

102

Religion is as much part of man as the love of beauty; it is part of his mind, and the mind is man himself knowing the world and his relation to it. It is therefore something real, for reality cannot be confined to what Bishop Berkeley's opponents discovered by stubbing their toes against stones or walls, and even that kind of reality is, in the end, made what it is through the mind. The reality of the mind is that which controls and defines the reality of the senses; it is both more profound and more wide-ranging, and it is in the end the true reality, for it contains both. We can know only through the perfect marriage of body and mind. The body informs, the mind knows, and neither is conceivable without the other. To describe religion as a psychosomatic projection of desires or anxieties is merely to assert an opinion, and to try to reduce knowledge to sense-data and pure perceptual experimentalism, while without the mind one can know neither what sense-data or perceptions are nor what they mean. If parts of the right side of the brain do not work, no amount of scratching and pin-pricking on the left leg or arm will be felt. Religion is supposed to be, by some, an illusion—but an illusion of what? Of a reality which cannot be probed or reached, or of the mind deceiving itself by creating a reality which does not exist?

The assertion that the reality created by the mind does not exist is merely an assertion by those who do not believe in it, or who believe that because there is nothing that can be scientific-ally measured and defined, and logically demonstrated or rejected, it does not exist. To put the problem in such terms is to reduce it either to a question of opinion or to an elementary syllogism of which the major premiss is: 'everything that exists must be apprehensible to the senses', and of which the con-clusion is that whatever is not so does not exist. But the mind is not apprehensible to the senses, and try as one may, one cannot define it or measure it, and no means have been found of making one. The fact is that the human mind has, since its existence, conveyed to the human being, in varying forms, the idea of the supernatural, which, somehow, gives meaning to his life and death, while nothing else does. This idea might be an illusion, for those who have no need or urge for it, but then it is an illusion in the same way as water is death for him who is forced to swallow it as part of tortures, and life for him who is dying of thirst in the desert. Those who are not thirsty should not drink, but they have no business to tell those who are thirsty not to drink, or that what they drink is not water but illusion. Perhaps it is so; there are indeed mirages in deserts, but there are cases when even mirages are heaven, and those who are in their comfortable houses have no ground for decrying them. There is no rationality in trying to prevent thirsty people from drinking if they can and want to; to do so merely shows a dog-in-the-manger attitude of spite towards something one does not need or cannot understand, or, as is often the case, an attitude of fear about the limitations of reason, or fear of being wrong: if one is afraid of being wrong, one wants to be so with as many people as possible, for there is a feeling of safety in numbers.

God, if God there is, cannot make a miracle for every man so as to convince him of His existence; neither is He possessed of attributes that scientifically minded man could verify and accept as valid or reject as invalid. God is nowhere to be found, no rocket can reach Him. He either is, in our minds and hearts, or He is not; He is therefore a reality of the mind, as the categorical imperative is a reality of the mind, not because it can be demonstrated as true; for, true to what? The question is impossible, since it could only be true to itself, something which cannot be verified, since it is merely a tautology. God is a reality of the mind, true to the kind of life and death which His existence makes for man, and of course He cannot be brought into it, wilfully, as one can bring into it varying degrees of scientific, historical or social knowledge. He must become part of our mind of His own free will, He must come into it by Himself, for the mind cannot wilfully bring Him in, if He is not in already. Does this mean that man cannot be made responsible as to whether he believes or not, and as to whether he rejects or accepts the idea and presence of God? In a certain sense, it is obviously so, in the sense that no amount of swotting mathematics will make an Einstein out of a dunce, and no amount of training will turn a five-foot weed into a rival for Mohammed Ali.

We all have certain aptitudes for this or that, for swimming underwater or climbing mountains, and we can either improve on them or make the best of what we have. We can't all be St Francis or St Teresa, but we can, if we feel the urge or the need, take a leaf from both, and listen for the hush of footsteps in the night. To do that, we must feel the need or the urge to listen. And here is the rub: how does one feel such a need or such an urge, and, first of all, should one feel it—'should' being here understood in the ethical sense, meaning that it might be good for us or for society to have such an urge or need? How should one proceed? There is no magic formula to act as a guide, no book of rules to follow, and even to talk of the latter one would need to be oneself convinced that to guide people in a given direction is good for them. That is also a problem, for how can we know what is good for others, how can we be convinced that what seems good for us is good for others, and that because we are happy in the state in which we are, we must turn to proselytism and ask others to follow us, so as to share in the same happiness? But the others are not ourselves; they are very different from us, and we cannot know them, therefore cannot advise them according to interests and longings that we cannot possibly assess. The choice must be entirely individual; everybody must decide by himself in the light of his needs and his longings.

In the man who is perfectly satisfied with life, who is a perfectly full bucket, there is neither room nor need for any additional drop, but if he is not so, if he is for ever at a cross-roads wondering where to go, if he cannot find peace in his actions and a sense of purpose and fulfilment in his life, then unless he loves his narcissism, his perplexities and suffering, he should, or at least it is reasonable to think that he might, look around for ways of getting out of such states. He might think of medicine or psychiatry, or he might turn towards using his own mind to try and see if he could elicit some glimmers of wisdom out of it. This would place his mind in a state of receptivity through which some answers might come, but these answers can come only from the mind connecting with its source—Being, and recognising in it the cause of its being and its finality. The whole operation of discovering the reality of Being or God is necessarily entirely personal, non-scientific and non-logical, and therefore this reality, which is subjective, cannot be dismissed as illusion by anyone who has not himself subjectively experienced it deeply and then rejected it. Those who have never experienced it have no moral basis for using the word 'illusion' about it, for they behave like people who try to pay for bought goods with coins which have no value or currency. Goods and currency are as much part of a closed system as subjective or transcendental reality and illusion. Material reality itself is illusion for many philosophers or religious leaders, from Buddha and Plato to Bishop Berkeley, but leaving that aside, the important question remains as to what reality truly is and how one can define it, and this question is nowhere near a definite or a satisfactory answer. Yet one thing is certain, reality cannot be confined to matter and sense-data, and Kant's distinction between the experimental world and the world of *a priori* synthetic judgments which is that of metaphysics, must always be kept in mind.

Can we know what a tree is without knowing anything about the earth into which it plunges its roots, about the air it breathes, and the water which it uses as the sap of life to feed its boughs, fruit and leaves? One could, no doubt, have a schematic idea of what a tree is from a photograph, from a painting or a mental picture conveyed through words, but one could not know what a tree is without knowing something of the world to which it belongs and from which it derives the elements of fire, water, earth and air that give it life. Life is wholeness and otherness; we are nothing without others. Everything that makes man is the result of contacts with, and the presence of, others, and we only move away from the narrow field of our individual desires and needs, towards the wider field in which they conflict or meet with those of others, so as to be led out of ourselves, towards the true reality which underlies human life and makes it what it is. This reality is the meeting-point of multiplicity, the one centre where infinites fuse and complete one another in love. Any look around us, beyond our own blinkers, necessarily leads us towards others, and the other can only be understood, not as an object to satisfy our needs, but as a subject with needs and longings like ours and those of other subjects, which form the texture of life as a transcendence of subjects, a vast spider's web of being,

106

ceaselessly woven by, and connected with, informing Being. Life viewed from such a level can bear neither the head-shaking attitude and groans of those who proclaim it absurd, nor the superficial attitude of the hedonist, nor the pessimism of those who look upon it as a mere vale of sorrows. It stands out, on the contrary, as a whole in which all the conflicting aspects are reconciled, beyond our understanding and finitude, into the creativeness of being which embraces the good and the bad, joys and sorrows, for the one would be meaningless without the other.

Man is born with certain mental structures and aptitudes for knowledge, but he is not born with his mind fully stored up with knowledge, though he is possessed of all the instinctual knowledge necessary to his survival, and of the memory of his millenary past where lies his undying awareness of Being. The newly born human animal does not need to be taught how to suckle his mother. He automatically finds the life-giving breast with his eyes shut, and the gesture brings him a satisfaction, a sense of security and comfort that he never forgets, not even on the brink of the grave, where his last thought is likely to be for his mother—womb of life and death. The human being cannot know whence he comes and where he goes, but he has a vague awareness of it, and he lives in unease until, through at-tention towards Being, he receives some answer to his readiness to receive one. The readiness may not be given, but it can be achieved by doing a minimum for it, given the initial impulse to do so. One may have an innate aptitude for maths or music, but one must also practise them in order to develop such an aptitude. I shall not proffer Pascal's advice, for I do not believe in mechanical kneeling in order to bring God to us; but I do believe that knowledge requires symbols and guiding beacons in order to unfold and develop, and that, therefore, if one feels the urge to know something about the meaning of life, this meaning will not be found in books on, say, biology or anthropology; it can only be found or suggested in the life of spirit, best embodied in the great avatars of the Divine, like Buddha, Christ and the great saints and sufis.

The life of Christ, whether we look upon him as divine or as a man of unique genius, offers perhaps the best way to open the mind to the true mystery of life, and a sustained reflection and meditation on this mystery might make possible the emergence of some glimmers of light illumining a reality which, once glimpsed, will never cease to fill the mind and the heart, in life and in death. Once such a visitation has taken place, life becomes different, though of course never reduced to the simplistic certitudes and satisfactions propounded by the opponents of faith, but, on the contrary, more than ever open to doubts and uncertainties as to what one should do or not do, and, above all, as to the importance of the lives of other people who, by their impact on ours, determine what we are in time and beyond time. To believe is not to take sleeping pills so as to doze through life and death, or drugs that would make us see life as a rosy dream, but, on the contrary, to be always tensely awake to today and to tomorrow, made of today and yesterday, as eternity is made through time, in which the body plays as important a part as the spirit, for the Incarnation testifies to it and sanctifies it, and the Resurrection stresses its vital role as a living thing, and not as a cloak to be rejected like an old snake-skin, once it has had its use through life. Body and soul form a whole, in the same way as matter and energy form a whole; they cannot be dissociated for, as Master Eckhart said: 'The soul will save itself only with the body that has been assigned to it.'

Christianity began by being an other-worldly religion dominated by Platonism, neo-Platonism and Augustinianism, and it remained more or less so right up to the thirteenth century, with the rise of rationalism and the scientific attitude fertilised by acquaintance with Greek and Islamic science. Truth until then could be reached only through the mediation of the Divine, or the Platonic Idea; it was, therefore, deductive and syllogistic. Everything had to be deduced from the Idea or the logos, and the world was looked upon as an image of God or a reflection or shadow of the Idea. Human reality grew in importance, the family began to assert itself as a vital unit, the mother's role increased on earth, as well as in heaven, and the virgin mother became more and more the intercessor between man and God, for after all God became man through her. Creation in all its aspects became more and more important, and the Franciscans, with their Blakean notion that everything in nature is holy and partakes of the Divine, fostered the emergence of philosophic realism. With it, all things were informed with essence, and knowledge did not come from the Idea as with Plato, or directly from the Divine as with Augustine, but started from things themselves informed with the Divine. Knowledge began with the senses and with perceptions, and Duns Scotus, Abelard, Roger Bacon, John of Salisbury, William of Ockham and other Franciscan monks inaugurated the notion of experimental science which, from then on, went from strength to strength.

Aristotelian rationalism re-emerged with Thomism, which soon became the dominant philosophico-theological attitude, until 1277, when the Sorbonne condemned some of Aquinas's theories and some aspects of Aristotelian rationalism. The ensuing brief revival of mysticism and the Augustinian belief that the truth involves God through His Church, or through the Scriptures, did not last for long. Religious truth became more and more a question of personal relation with God; Ockham insisted on the moral obligation of following conscience and one's sincere beliefs. Knowledge started from phenomenal reality and the senses, and, most important of all, reason did not contradict faith but led to faith. This philosophical realism was stronger in the North of France than in the South, and Gothic art was obviously more realistic than Norman art, which remained more Augustinian and Platonic, with its love of lines and geometrical figures. It was the scientific attitude of realism of the Franciscan order that lay at the root of the great discoveries in all domains, and not, as is often said, the Renaissance which was essentially Platonistic. Da Vinci shared in the Platonic love of ideal beauty, and harmony of geometrical lines, but his experimentalism, his enquiring mind and his continuous search for the laws of nature and for new discoveries, related him to Copernicus, Francis Bacon, Galileo and the Positivists who followed. The love of things Greek and of Platonism in the various Renaissances which took place between the thirteenth and the sixteenth centuries did not affect the Christian spirit dominating the artistic and social life of these ages. Platonism only supplied the appearances in some cases, but the spirit remained profoundly Christian. The spiritual beauty of the 'Madonna of the Rocks' comes from the Christian world, and not from the Attic shores.

'If one deprives oneself of the benefit of mathematics, one is left with doubts, opinions and errors', said Roger Bacon in the thirteenth century, and Da Vinci in the fifteenth: 'Things that have not passed through the senses are empty, do not participate in life'; and it was Da Vinci who said, four centuries before Bergson: 'Nothingness is the most important thing in the concept of time; it finds itself between the past and the future without possessing anything of the present.' Those who wish to divide history, art, literature or thought into watertight compartments, epochs, structures or whatever one likes, one fitting with the other like the vast slabs that bear the continents of the earth, are bound to have a hard task. The mind is never possessed, except in the case of obsessions and mental disorders, by one single thought or attitude, and history can never be summed up by one single spiritual attitude. In the seventeenth century, the realism of Protestantism, of Rembrandt, Vermeer or Le Nain is balanced by the Platonism of Racine and Poussin, just as the neo-classicism of the end of the eighteenth century and the beginning of the nineteenth is balanced by the individualism of Romanticism. Hegel, who partakes of both attitudes and synthetises both by fusing real and rational, stated that the Incarnation is the crux of Christianity and the foundation of universal history. This makes it clear that God is only God if man and creation recognise Him as God and return His love to Him, and it stresses also the importance of time. God is immanent in creation, He is among men, and spiritually partakes of all the aspects of their lives, thus firmly disposing of the manichean notion that the body is one thing and the soul or spirit another.* In spite of neo-Platonic influences, Christianity is basically existential, permeated with the Hebraic sense of the importance of history and time; it is essentially activity, God's activity intent upon spiritualising matter so that He may finally know Himself in perfection. Man

---

*The doctrine that matter is intrinsically evil and the source of Evil is wholly un-Platonic. Plato, in *The Laws*, ascribes evil to disorderly motions of the soul.

partakes of this activity and is the means by which it is carried out. His consciousness, his mind, issued from and connected with Being, contain the image and the coded knowledge of the universe, and progressively unravel it, until he and the universe will be one in the absolute knowledge of Being.

8

Some Aspects of Love

The notion of the oneness of body and spirit is vital to ethics and to the problem of love and sex. Materialism is naturally hedonistic, and the pleasure principle and the satisfaction of one's desires, instincts and appetites is what matters. Dualism between matter and spirit results either in attaching no importance whatsoever to the satisfaction of the body, or in confining it to the life of the instincts and animal pulsions, while the mind is made the seat of the spirituality which tries to control it, without being affected by it. The body can either be looked upon as the fount of all corruptions and the source of constant dangers to the soul, or it can be progressively controlled and shorn of its desires, as in Buddhism, which looks upon it as an impediment to ultimate beatitude, and therefore aims at getting rid of it once and for all, so as never to return to what Yeats called 'the fury and the mire of human veins'.

If the body is used as an instrument of sensuous pleasure, without any moral feelings involved, it becomes an object, and he who uses it becomes also an object, for he who indulges in purely physical pleasures is bound to lose the consciousness of his subjectivity. In this case, the intensity and the extent of the pleasure derived from the body are the only criteria of the relationships involved, which are above all a question of instruments and of technique. A young and beautiful body, and a certain amount of technical knowledge of the mechanics of love-making on both sides, will achieve much better results than total inexperience—unless of course this inexperience is suffused with true love which transforms everything. Needless to say, this type of mechanical relationship and performance has nothing to do with love. It is pure and simple erotic satisfaction practised often enough, since mankind acquired enough leisure and well-being to indulge in it—that is to say, strangely enough, since the dawn of civilisation.

Sex is, of course, part of love, but it is not coequal with love. Love between two people of opposite sexes necessarily includes sex, while sex does not necessarily include love. Two people of opposite sexes can love each other without any sexual relations, if this is impossible because of some physical impediment or social barrier, but whether there is sexual consummation or not, there certainly is a mental sexual relationship, and the mind, as Blake pointed out, is more important than the body, for, as Christ said, 'Whosoever looketh on a woman to lust after her hath committed adultery with her already in his heart.' (*Matthew*, V, 28) Emotional impurity is at least as destructive for the human person as bodily impurity. The range and profundity of any sexual relationship are determined by the imagination and the affective involvement of the participants. If they are truly in love with each other, then the sexual act is an act of communion and a conscious and subconscious attempt by each of them to merge totally in the fulfilment of the other. Love is the giving of oneself as a subjective self, and the means of unifying body and mind with another subjective self, with whom one finds oneness and the perfection of living and of dying. Sex, then, is the expression, and also the culmination, of a physical and spiritual relationship which has the beauty of immanent mysticism, thus reducing duality to oneness. It has about it an aura of sacredness which no social conventions can affect or deflect, for it carries with it the capacity of transcending them through death. Though it is true to say that the life of mankind is not entirely made up of such exalted relationships, there are enough examples of this type to illumine the way for others, and there are enough people who, according to their own imaginative and affective range, love each other, if not with the intensity and absoluteness of the most famed archetypes of love, certainly with the conviction of persons who are aware that their spiritual integrity and beauty depend on the purity of their motives and of the bonds which unite them to the one whom they have chosen as the complement of their true being.

The expression 'to have sex' unavoidably associates sex with

114

mechanicalness, and with a kind of merchandise which can be had for the asking, or the buying. To make love necessarily includes love, and as such the sexual act is part of the beauty of love itself, as a giving of oneself to another. Beauty—physical or aesthetic—cannot be defined; it is an imaginative insight into the true reality of things, a kind of illumination which causes a feeling of harmony within oneself and with the being of creation. Beauty in the human being is not specifically a question of regular features and perfectly shaped body, though of course these attributes can only enhance the person who already possesses that other strange and indefinable emanation called beauty. Greta Garbo did not possess Greek features or the body of a Venus, yet she was most beautiful when she conveyed the truth of love, because she made everyone want to love her. Marilyn Monroe possessed the same quality; she had physical beauty, but she had, above all, a special gift or emanation connected with sex, which immediately awoke men's imagination, vitality and desires. There are many women more beautiful than she was, but, lacking that special gift, their impact on men and on women is considerably reduced.

Sex, as part of love, is a means of communication more moving than speech; it is body and mind speaking as one a language which can only be apprehended and echoed by another body-and-mind unit, perfectly attuned with it. Sex by itself, cocktail sex, post-prandial sex, sex as satisfaction of an itch, as the rubbing together of two skins, or as the fusion and exhaustion of two animal pulsions, neither requires nor carries any affective and spiritual ties or experience. At most, it may happen that either of the partners dreams of someone else while using the other in order to play his or her little piece of music. It can be a pleasurable form of passing the time, for those who have time and are mentally and ethically equipped for it, but it can neither be treated as love nor, of course, can it be practised by all. Those who feel and think with their body as well as with their mind—and such are the normal laws of life—are too aware of the fact that the body has its own purity, its own sincerity and its own truth, which can neither be faked nor mocked. Few people go through life without ever giving a thought to the import or the truth of their actions, but even those who don't are nevertheless marked by their actions and by their refusal to weigh and to examine their causes and their worth, for the mind is fed by the senses, which consciously or subconsciously record their impact on it, and shape it. A purely sexual relationship, that is to say a relationship which aims at purely physical pleasure, is not something that could be looked upon as bringing a spiritual satisfaction and enlightenment to any man. It is not very different from the pleasure derived from a good meal; there is nothing in it which could be universalised and advocated as morally elevating and ennobling, and, whether one likes it or not, man is an inherently moral animal, an animal which can think of tomorrow, and one cannot hope for very bright tomorrows if one's criteria for life are good meals and varied sexual relations, probably followed, as in the decadent days of Rome, by vomiting for those who wish to go on eating, and by massage and baths for those who wish to go on copulating.

The Church has for long confused sex and love, and alas, partly continues to do so. Sex has been for centuries an ugly word, and chastity has been held up as a noble ideal. Chastity can be an ideal only for those who have very special dispositions for it. Chastity transcended into spiritual activities which spread the love of life is good, but chastity which results in frustrations and warped attitudes towards the positiveness and exuberance of life is not a virtue, and it ought to be discouraged because it causes priggishness in the person who practises it, and resentment and negativeness in those who are in contact with it. Chastity implies emotional purity, that is to say total emotional sincerity with oneself and with others, for without it there cannot be any true love relationship, and therefore any true claim to real chastity. At the animal level, sex is dominated by the pleasurable instinct of reproduction, pleasurable because, if it were not so, there would not be any reproduction, but with man it cannot be reduced merely to that, though it can embrace that as part of the will to the continuation of life. Sex is not an ugly word in itself, for it is beautiful as part of true love, in which it becomes a means of creation and transformation. The tension that fuses two beings together into oneness must be spiritual as well as physical, for neither can be complete without the other, and

116

one cannot truly love someone without feeling the intense sensual urge to commune with him or with her, and thus to reduce separateness to a duality of essences, turning for a timeless moment otherness into the positiveness of being. Such moments of union and total affective truth are, when they take place, unforgettable, and they leave their indelible mark on the body as well as on the mind. They can be emulated, but they cannot be repeated; and those who have experienced them can never again approach a similar experience without summoning from memory the awareness of this unique reality, which necessarily casts its shadow on whatever brings it to consciousness, thus rendering everything of a similar nature intolerable, or at least deeply affected by it, in the same way as a great light renders invisible all smaller lights. The experience of true love is not repeatable; for Iseult there is only one Tristan, and for Juliet there is only one Romeo. The truth of the poetic mind is the real truth; poets have charted, through the imagination, the range of human consciousness, and they have shown that once the level of essence has been reached, repetition is not possible; it would be indeed a repetition of the same, and identity cannot be repeated. The experience of oneness of essences once reached necessarily stands, like a fire, at the centre of the two beings who have undergone it, and anything which is of a similar nature and which comes near enough to the heart of its truth is consumed by it and becomes it.

The love of God implies, as previously stated, total selflessness and receptivity for absorption into Being, an absorption which is not a total disappearance of individuated essence but a means for individuated essence to become conscious of its true identity, through Being, which informs it. Brotherly love is sacred, because it flows from the nature of Being which is love, and it aims at unifying the whole of mankind into the oneness of love; it rests upon the awareness that the neighbour, the other, is an individuated essence, part of creation, submitted to the same needs, and suffering the same limitations, the same disasters like disease, wars and earthquakes, and the same end which is death. It is only by loving a human being through God, or through some transcendental notion which raises him to the level of indestructibility and identity with us in perenniality and reality, that we can love him unconditionally for what he is and not for what we can make of him. To 'love thy neighbour as thyself' does not seem to be much good, for there is no vital reason for loving oneself as oneself. There are even plenty of reasons for not loving oneself, for such a love is barren and finally self-destructive.

To love is to love the other as the other, as God's creature, a burden upon God as we are, and as such, because of our common transcendental fate, all the more worthy of love, without any of the restrictions that one could apply to the love of self. For if one must condemn one's weaknesses and endeavour to mend them, one must never condemn outright those of others. Our only moral duty is to try to understand them, and to love men as Christ loved them, not because they are good or bad, but because they are men. One must love in man not so much what he can give as what makes him God's creature, for however dark the night might be, there is not a man, unless he is completely out of his mind, who has not, every now and then, dreams or glimmers of the absent or coming light. If he had not, he would be in hell, in a world of total despair, and he would more than ever need our sympathy for having been so totally deprived of his humanity. But we must not forget that darkness is part of light, as much as nothingness is part of being, and that we do not discover God either by staring at the horizon or gazing upward, but by shutting our eyes and listening, as St John of the Cross did in his 'noche obscura', for the dawning of the Divine is always preceded by night.

To love the unlovable is not easy, though we must try, for by loving the other we help him to bear his burden of sorrows or of disharmony with himself, and we contribute thus to the establishment of oneness and harmony in mankind. But just as communion with Being does not mean total obliteration into Being, oneness with mankind does not mean total loss of individuality or identity to a greater unit. Neither Hegel nor Marx, who are often wrongly credited with such notions, ever advocated the disappearance of the individual into the whole. True, according to them, the individual can fulfil himself only by working for the good of society and not for himself, but Christianity does not say anything very different from that, and

Kant's categorical imperative, on the plane of ethics, binds individual action to similar laws, advocating the universalisation of individual experience and behaviour. Knowledge is individual, and always results from a subject knowing the laws of nature, or knowing himself through observation or through objects fused into his own experience, which at the level of pure subjectivity reaches the universal. But no man has ever been, or will ever be, the same as another, therefore there are bound to be conflicts and misunderstandings or lack of understanding, which are a necessary part of life. It is important to try never to lose sight of the essential traits that are part of the human condition, and therefore to try always to temper human individualism with awareness of the other's needs, which cannot be met through hostility or aggression.

The dialectic of existential conflict is without any ontological foundations, and it cannot bring about any fruitful results, either between individuals or between nations. Six thousand years of history make this point clear, as they make clear the fact that the more elaborate and destructive the weapons of war become, the more it becomes vital to ban their use, which would only lead to catastrophic disasters and to suffering such as would totally transform the life of man. Reason, which is the essence of man, should be the light by which all conflicts— individual or international—are resolved, so that men can hop as best they can along the path that leads them from birth to death. Their journey will be easier, more true to man's essence which is love, if they discard selfishness and false rationalisations of their desires and appetites so as to blame others, and, on the contrary, look upon their travelling companions as brothers and not as enemies.

Man needs friends, and friendship, at varying levels, is necessary to man. Friendship at the highest level, at the level at which it is something practically unique in any man's life, is difficult to realise; this belongs to the realm of affective affinities, and resolution of opposites and differences into a harmony or equilibrium that images and reflects divine love. Friendship is an opening of the heart and the mind, seeking echoes and responses from someone else with whom one is essentially attuned. It can take place between people of the same sex, or, more rarely, between people of opposite sexes; but in the latter case there is always a certain amount of sexuality involved, unless the protagonists are old or asexuated, or unless either of them is protected from sexual connotations by a taboo which cannot be overcome; this taboo could be love for another person, or a religious taboo.

Friendship is a choice, but a choice ruled by laws that are inherent in it. It cannot be willed, it cannot be imposed on someone who does not want it, and it cannot have any other end except its own which is disinterested love. If it is a relationship established in order to achieve a purpose that is not disinterested love, then it falls within the categories so admirably described by La Rochefoucauld as various disguises of self-interest. If one desires one's own satisfaction or good, the other through whom one reaches such a goal is merely an instrument, an object, but not a subject, part of a relationship for giving and taking, and for reconciling all in the harmony of love. The essential good or value of any living being is his freedom, his freedom to be himself, to give himself to whomever or whatever he chooses to be his supreme spiritual good or value, be it the good itself or another human being. If he is deprived of his choice, that is to say of what he takes to be the exercise of his freedom, he ceases to be a man and becomes a thing with no purpose and finality of its own—something worse than death, which has a purpose and a finality. The choice, therefore, must be free, and once made, it must be upheld with truth and sincerity, for it commits both the maker and the object of the choice, which reflects responsibility on to the chooser. Friendship is not possible without the complete spiritual equality of the partners, whatever the differences in ideas, beliefs or social status, and the complete lack of subordination of the one to the other, or desire of the one either to please or to use the other. Any friendship that contains such notions is corrupt, and is more an association of interests than a union of two subjects, who must always remain two and not try to be one. Oneness is only possible with God, or in pure moments of union between man and woman, bound by true love. The essential basis for friendship is respect for the other's autonomy, whatever the respective age or intellectual standing of the two partners. Friendship does not presuppose any other equality except metaphysical equality, it means that friends view all problems that separate or unite them in the light of a love which transcends all differences and is in conformity with the true nature of love which is to relate the individual to God, or to transcendence. In fact, the respect for the total autonomy of the other is the vital basis for human relations in all domains, on the affective as well as the political plane. The individual must always be allowed space around him and distance, so as to remain what he truly is. Fusion in human relations, as well as in politics, is a destruction of personality, which results in hatred and in the violence that is called forth in order to deal with it. No human relation is valid that does not rest upon consent. Union for a common ideal or purpose is positive and enriching; unity under one single enforced rule is a soul-destroying master-slave relationship.

Parental love rests not upon consent, but upon necessity, and upon the recognition of the rationality and universality of this necessity. A father or a mother must necessarily love the children whom they have brought into the world. They are responsible for having drawn them out of non-being into being, and for having endowed them with a body and a mind which will submit them to all the ups and downs of life. They are therefore morally bound to look after them, until they have reached the age when they can look after themselves. The fact that a child does not behave according to his parents' dreams or wishes, or does not respond to their kindness and generosity, is no reason to reject him or to withdraw love from him. First of all, what looks like kindness and generosity from the parents' side may well look like intolerable interference and possessiveness from the child's side. But more important than this question of respective interpretations of attitudes and behaviour is the fact that love is and must be a gratuitous gift, and not something given in return for something else. This is commerce or barter, in the course of which a given commodity is exchanged for another. To love is to give freely without restriction or conditions; otherwise, it is calculation in order to obtain something in return.

121

If parents are morally bound to love their children, children ought to love their parents, who naturally feel the need for such a love, in the same way as they may feel the need for food. Therefore if it does not come, pain and moral suffering are caused; yet if it does not come of its own volition, it cannot be forced or bribed by any kind of action. It must come naturally and spontaneously, as an expression of joy and gratitude for life. The way to kill any feeling is to insist upon it, to demand it, or to try to remonstrate with the one from whom one expects it. Love can never be given out of some moral or physical compulsion. If a watched kettle never boils, wanted love never comes. But the categorical imperative about love necessarily applies to love as the natural response of a freely chosen responsibility such as parenthood. In such a case, love is a duty, and it cannot be refused or withheld without denying the principle of freedom, for a child who is not loved by his parents is necessarily handicapped, and partly deprived, at the start, of his freedom and his aptitude for living. A father's duty is to love all his children, the good and the bad, and he cannot discriminate between them without replacing the moral law by individual egoism, which is immoral and contrary to God's law.

God loves all men, the good and the bad, and as the good find their own satisfaction in their being good, that is to say in being entirely in conformity with their essence, He devotes more attention to the bad than to the good, for He suffers, or He is deeply affected, by their being so far away from Him. Yet He cannot intervene without turning the human creature into a puppet, and creation itself into a toy for His own amusement, and that would be a denial of the essence of being which is freedom within Being. So every creature must find his way to His will through his free will, which, as an emanation of being, can be free only when it coincides with being.

Parents must be tolerant towards their child's failings, and that for two reasons. The first, already mentioned, is that they are responsible for his birth and therefore ultimately for his death too; the second is that, being older, and having already lived through the stages the child is now living through, they ought to have more experience and more wisdom than their child, and it is always the duty of those who know more to understand and to forgive those who know less. It is easy to yield to impulses and to dismiss someone as being unlovable, but it is indeed the unlovable who should be loved, for they obviously are most in need of it, even if or because they profess to disdain it. One cannot rationally decide whether so and so deserves or does not deserve to be loved; one never possesses the required knowledge to pass such judgments; only God could do so, and God, Who knows best, does not do so. He advises us to love everyone as we would like to be loved; He does not set out any standards or criteria in the name of which love should be given, withheld or rationed. The moral duty is to love, and if we decide to withhold our love from someone on the assumption that he does not deserve it, we commit both an act of pride and an act of niggardliness by not giving something that could help another human being; we behave, in fact, in a self-centred way, so as to please ourselves, even though we rationalise our behaviour by blaming the other.

This does not mean that love must be showered indiscriminately and equally on all human beings, the good and the bad; some are certainly more conducive to love than others. It is obvious that Joan of Arc is more lovable than her contemporary Gilles de Rais, and as such, she will elicit a direct, spontaneous response of love: yet Gilles de Rais also is in need of love, not for what he did, but for the sadness caused by the wastage and distortion of so much of God-made creation, turned into a total negation of God's essence, which is the love of the other. One might call the type of love called forth by him and his like compassion for the afflicted, the weak or the wicked, who inflict torments and shame upon themselves as well as upon man in general. Every fallen creature, whatever his faults, is entitled as a human being—and nothing, no one but God can deprive him of his humanity—to the love or the compassion of his fellow beings. Punishment itself must not exclude compassion, otherwise it becomes sadism; it must always be mitigated with sadness and a twinge of the heart which every human being worthy of the name must necessarily experience at the sight of another human being behaving in a cruel or monstrous way which diminishes both mankind and its Creator.

The Eichmanns of this world should call forth more sadness, terror and ontological compassion than hatred or violence towards them, for they are the obverse of man, and they show

123

by their behaviour that man is widening the gap between himself and God, Who has to make a much greater effort of appetition and therefore of essence to bring such men back to Him than He has to make for a good man. The hatred and violence of those who have directly suffered at the hands of Eichmann is understandable, and cannot be lightly dismissed by those who have not endured, as they have, not so much personal suffering as the loss of dear ones, something which is far more difficult to bear than one's own suffering. Compassion in punishment must not become blindness or a blanket response to all sorts of evil. Evil is not ontological, but social, therefore society must devise humane and rational means of dealing with it. Vengeance, the eye-for-an-eye attitude, does not come within this category. Eichmann would probably have suffered more, if ever suffering was the retributive element sought for suffering and destruction caused, if he had been allowed to live, rather than being given instead a swift death. Above all, he would have contributed more to the widening of human conscience, including his own, and to the spreading of the awareness of the crimes committed and the terrible insult to God and man, if he had been given long years of life so that both he and mankind had plenty of time to see and to weigh all the imports of his crimes, and by truly repenting of them, to add to the eternal essence and to God's self-knowledge. Death is not the best way to redeem man or society; life is far more painful, more instructive and, in cases of moral or physical abjection, more difficult to bear.

9

The Need for Light

Being, cause of being and time, keeps on making itself felt and causes individuated being to be torn between love of life and existence in time, and reunion with Being, through the abolition of individuation and multiplicity, and return to the one—the still point of darkness and light whence it came. Individuated being longs for oneness, and fears the loss of being which will reduce it to a state of non-being and total knowing, excluding all longings or sense of absence, since it is both absence and presence in one. Time is part of the dialectic of eternity, the means by which it turns from pure transparency into a mirror in which it can look at itself making its perfection and knowing itself as perfection. God is the being of creation, and He has as many ways and languages as time and place require, through which He speaks or whispers to human creatures. All men, from the beginning of creation to its end, are part of His concern, and He calls them all, though not all can hear Him or see Him. Many do not hear Him at all, and some can only faintly hear the hush of His voice, or see vague glimmers of His presence; some go to Him through barely trodden paths, or even entirely by themselves, others through the broad avenues of church guidance; yet none is privileged in comparison with others. In His eyes, what counts is that men should hear Him and come to Him, and as for those who do not, He always expects them as one expects an absent guest, and He suffers from their absence. Those who are with Him have no easier a time than those who are away from Him; they are never sure that the light they are seeing will last, for faith is neither security nor certainty. Christ himself at times found his uncertainty difficult to bear, and he asked questions that remained unanswered, or rather they were answered by silence, which meant that he had to obey and perform his appointed task.

Faith is neither a life-long guarantee for unfailing good behaviour, with salvation at the end of it, nor a force to keep the believer constantly on the path of perfect goodness. It is only an aspiration towards it, and a hope for the eternal presence of God's love. It is, like all things human, a flickering light which at times burns bright and at times splutters and even fades out; and man can never know whether the grace and love that sustain it will be strong enough to maintain it in being. The Church includes both saints and sinners—all men, who are neither perfect nor fixedly unchanging through time. Therefore, the Church as an institution must be able to modify its phenomenal aspect in conformity with the changing sensibility and mental attitudes of its members, so that God may speak to them in terms which they can understand. But the noumenal aspect of the Church, the core of beliefs and doctrines upon which it rests, must remain unchanged and unaffected by whatever forms liturgy or appearances may take.

Whether church music is played on organs or on guitars, or whether the priest faces the altar or the nave is of no great importance. Superficial transformations of church practices or attempted modernisations of the life of Christ will not contribute a jot to true faith. The Church is not a place of entertainment to be filled up at all costs. The people who come to be entertained do not come because they believe in God, and faith in God's love for mankind can be maintained only by renewing, not its appearances, but its spirituality. The appearance is only the beggar's rags, hiding his immortal soul and his bodily mortality. The Church must therefore concern itself with the true presence of Christ in all earthly actions, and in the constant communion, through his love, between God and man. Christ alone is eternal, in time and beyond time, and the Church—his creation—is eternal only in its spiritual identification with him, through his essential and subsistent spirituality, but neither as an institution nor, of course, through its members. That is why the good or bad conduct of Popes, bishops, priests or church-goers is no reason for condemning or praising the Church as a whole. Its worth should be measured not by its failings and its follies, like the Inquisition, the

126

Crusades, the religious wars, the crimes of Torquemada, Borgia or other Popes and bishops, but by the achievements of two thousand years and by the lives of its saints or other love-motivated Christians. Christ, though he may suffer through every human weakness and crime, is neither destroyed nor altered by any. He remains Christ—God—spirit incarnated— the hope and longing of man, whatever the strength or weakness of his faith.

Christianity, as Christ made clear by his life and behaviour, is essentially a praxis, a means of redeeming the time, more wide-embracing and Pentecostal than Marx's vision of the New Jerusalem and the stateless state. Mother Teresa of Calcutta, St Francis, St François de Sales and all those who practise a Christian life of action have a greater impact on the life of mankind than those who, having encountered God, may think it enough to pray and go to church. Christianity is concern for the human creature in time, as the maker of eternity, and not a transitory stage in which to wait for eternity patiently or forbearingly. It was in as far as Christianity was escapism and denial of life that Marx could describe it as the opium of the people, but though such notions were quite widespread in his time, Western man now realises more and more that the essential teaching and life of Christ are against such interpretations, and that life—that 'tale told by an idiot, full of sound and fury, signifying nothing'—is a gift which affords man the total fulfilment of his body and mind. The body is as important as the mind; this will never be said enough, and creation is positiveness—through the triumph of the positive aspects of life over the negative, and the emergence, from the countless virtualities of existence, of those that have in themselves more positivity than others and are better equipped than others to achieve the complete fulfilment of their essence. Creation is not a throw of dice in the dark night of non-being; it is the result of the slow, yet unavoidable, coming together of elements that possess in themselves the necessary appetitions and complementarities to form living organic entities, as part of the living continuum of the changing universe.

Seen in terms of religion, creation is an act of love, not a gesture of despair or denial, and to construe the non-interference of God in it as a sign of forsakenness is to exhibit a lack of adulthood which cannot conceive of life except as a walk constantly hand in hand with Father. Father wants us to walk and to decide by ourselves. He has not given us freedom as a gift, locked up in some Pandora's box, or as a pair of scales with which to weigh what to do or not to do. He has made us free as He Himself is free, and therefore freedom is nowhere to be found in external reality or in the conceptual world; it exists only in our actions and thoughts, and we only know it through them. It is not something that we can pull out of our pockets or our minds and use in order to make our choices about an action which, since it does not exist yet, has not elicited the choice that could precede it and determine it. We know our freedom only by acting, by doing things, and once action has taken place; it is always therefore *a posteriori* knowledge, derived from our actions which, once performed, tell us whether they were free, that is to say in conformity with our own inner truth or essence, or unfree, that is to say fettered by egoism, ambition, instincts, socio-cultural conventions and habits, or purposes that have nothing much to do with the essential humanity of man. Freedom is a search for and adherence to the being of Being, and the saint is undeniably the best example of total freedom, for he endeavours to adhere, all the time, to the will of Being. Freedom is essentially epistemological, it is a way of knowing what we truly are, that is to say, what our ethos, made up of our instincts, our subconscious and conscious memories and our socio-cultural background, truly is, and we know that the further away we are from the ideals that make man man, the less free we are. These ideals are not abstractions, they are the light that must guide man's actions as part of history and creation.

Man cannot, except through escapism and illusionism, place himself out of time and history, and declare either that God is dead or that life is absurd. If God has ever been alive, He cannot be dead, and the only predicate that can be used with the word 'God' is the verb *to be* in the present affirmative. If the world is—and it certainly is, since, whether we like it or not, we are part of it—it is not absurd; it is what it is, and it is we who declare it absurd to suit our feelings or our morality, but we do not make it absurd by saying so. All we do is to exhibit a certain churlishness, not to say arrogance, which, because we do not get any answer to our exasperated questions, or because we cannot solve the problem of the origin and finality of creation through our own reason, declares that it is beyond reason or that there is no rationality in it. This, of course, affords us the self-satisfaction of injured pride and a kind of superficial dignity in which we wrap ourselves up, in order to play at being gods, since there is no God, and to triumph over the apparent absurdity of life through stoic pride. This may be a very satisfying feeling for anyone who is fit to experience it, but not for others, who rather call it priggishness and Olympian indifference to the suffering of those who cannot afford such flights, since they do not set themselves up as Prometheus defying the gods, but are merely men sweating at their work, or aching with illness in their beds. Yet it is they who truly matter, for they are not part of any man-made absurd cloud-world, but part of history which they themselves make through their actions, their suffering, their dreams, their failures, which may be described as absurd only by outsiders who look at them from the ivory tower of their imagination or from the moon. Yet one can live in an ivory tower only if other men attend to one's needs, and one cannot live for long on the moon, one has to come back to earth, among men, and realise that, however unwillingly, one is part of the historical reality that one denies or ignores, and that one cannot get out of it by trying to subsume all men's exertions under the grandiose abstraction of *man*, seen purely as an entity of the mind.

Man is man as a social and historical being; he is not free not to be so; he is the texture of society and history; he is condemned to his situation, and his true freedom is to live it so that he is as much as possible in accord with its purpose which is the perfect humanisation of man, to the point where he will cease being man and assume, by his behaviour and thought, the image of God. This requires action and not evasion, and a constant awareness of the concrete, the particular or lived reality, and a constant avoidance of the abstract and the general which make possible so much indifference and so much cruelty. If one replaces the living entity and individuality of man by labels such as Negro, Arab, German or Jew, then one can do whatever one likes with such abstractions, in the name of ends that justify any means used. But if man remains man, a living compound of good and evil, dreams, longings and failures, that is to say something that is the image, the replica of ourselves, then we have greater possibilities of treating him as a brother and accepting him as such, while trying to make him see, if he is a violent or greedy man, that his behaviour is inhuman, and should be modified so that he might apply to all around him the greatest human virtue, which is tolerance. 'History does nothing', said Marx, 'it is man, real living man who does everything . . . It is only man's activity in the pursuit of his own finality.'

Man is part of history, whether he consents to it or not; if he does not, he is part of the negating, escapist forces which have to be overcome, so that its positiveness and end may be realised. This end does not exist in advance, it is being made, and whether God exists or not, He does not intervene in it, He leaves it to man whose destiny it is to carry it out; this end will only be achieved, and therefore known for what it is, once man is no more, but has become it, as total self-knowledge. This end is transcendent to history, and it continuously manifests itself in it, and feeds the immanence which tends towards its realisation. How to discover this immanence is man's problem, which is not solved by saying that he is helpless, that suffering and death 'are incomprehensible', and that therefore all he can do is to wring his hands and curse or stare when he meets them or, stiff-lipped, pass coldly by. This is the kind of attitude that contributes to history in a negative way, as a stone lodged in the axle of a car prevents the wheels from turning at their normal speed; it does not stop the car, but it hampers it. 'Nous sommes engagés', said Pascal, we can only get on with it. Every stream either goes down to the sea or dries up on its way, and then goes to the sea via the clouds, but to the sea it goes, until, in the end, there will be no seas. We make history; let us therefore make it in the light of thoughts and beliefs that will turn it, not into a continuous feast, but at least into a bearable journey in which men will not kick those who fall down or stand in their way, but on the contrary help them, and stand side by side with them until we reach, and pass beyond, the end.

Non-mathematical or experimental truth, the truth of experience, cannot be mediated by churches, political parties or political or religious texts; this kind of truth can only be mediated as intersubjectivity apprehended by individual subjectivity. One can discover God only by turning away from things and looking into the silence of oneself as essence. 'Look into yourself', said St Augustine, 'for truth lies there.' No church or political party, with the inherent dogmatism that is part of any institution, whether religious or political, can bring about the salvation of mankind. Only love, true Christian love, which posits, above all things, the sacredness of life in time and out of time, and the importance of individuated being, informed with Being and part of it, can do that. This means that neither of these two vital principles can, on any account, be over-ridden, whether in the name of the future, the happiness of tomorrow, or the perenniality and authority of the Church or the party. Tomorrow is in the making, and no man can ask another, or some Iphigenia, to die so that favourable winds may lead to it. Churches and political parties have often carried out massive destructions of some of their members or opponents, for the so-called preservation of their integrity and purity which, according to them, transcends all other considerations. This has given rise, and still gives rise, to endless tyrannies and wanton destruction of human life. It proceeds from a deification of the institution, whether it is the Church or a party, which uses its dogma or God's name as a means to exercise cruelties and destruction that are totally alien to God or to the humanism that these parties preach.

The syllogistic argument has been throughout history an instrument of terror in the hands of fanatics who always manage to force or to smuggle in the acceptance of the premiss that opens the way to what looks like a rational enforcement of authority. Thus we have had inquisitions, Gulag Archipeligos, the expulsion of Garaudy and of any others who infringe the dogma of the party. No political or religious institution that does not have as a basic working principle the love of man and the sacredness of life can hope to bring about peace or prosperity in the world. It is obvious that no political or religious institution fully meets this requirement at this moment. The nation is the dominant political unit, and nationalism, whether it is socialist, Communist or liberal, is by far the most important force at work in the world. Neither Communism nor any number of international groupings for one purpose or another can disguise the fact that the national interest transcends all interests, in the same way as egoism tends to transcend all interests, unless it is counteracted by love for others. Yet the love of man cannot discriminate between Russians and Americans, capitalists and proletarians. It must include all men, irrespective of their creed, race and political opinions.

Any political system that rejects one part of society as alien to it is bound to be considerably hampered in its work by this non-integrated part of itself, and, in the end, to be destroyed by the combination of the violence of its resistance with the violence which the dominant system will have to display in order to keep it at bay or to destroy it. Divisions and separations necessarily create violence—the violence of the one who is rejected, and the violence of the one who rejects, and who can only maintain and finally assert his rejection through violence, which, in the end, becomes the dominant ethos of the society that has adopted such principles, and thus passes from one revolution to another, from one military ruling group to another. Violence necessarily deflects any political or religious creed towards authoritarianism and hierarchic structures in which the individual is always compelled to submit his judgment and well-being to the will of authority which, though it may invoke varying politico-economic creeds and shifts from one group to another, can only maintain its coercive institutions and autonomy by force. Therefore this authority can never reach a state of equilibrium and democratic stability; it always remains in a state of challenge and defence against antibodies which it tries to crush or reject, and this can only result in a system which, though ideologically different from the one overthrown, has the same structure of imbalance and inbuilt conflict, which will go on until exclusion is finally turned into integration, in the same way as Christ did not fight evil with violence, but absorbed it through the love and understanding that reunite and bring peace to all. The dialectics of alienation and rejection can only lead to violence and cyclical destruction. Therefore capitalists must not be looked on as poison to be eliminated, but as misguided people to be converted to more humane principles of social life; they must not be rejected, but made part of the new society, which cannot come into being through arrogance, whatever its basis, or through self-righteousness and intolerance.

There is no doubt that the corruption, the hypocrisies, egoism and lust for power and wealth of democratic societies are not half as inhuman and cruel as the total disregard for the individual which obtains in totalitarian states, either under Fascist or Communist rule. Anyone who is free from the complex which afflicts the guilt-ridden, mostly bourgeois-born left, who can only approach the sacred cow of Communism with eyes shut and obnubilated rationality, will be able to see that the cruelty towards, and the destruction of, the human person through brainwashing psychiatric treatment and tortures in asylums or in camps are much worse, much more degrading than all the weaknesses and naked egoism of the West, for, after all, in the West there is always the hope that men will either modify their ways through their own conscience, or be made to do so through the pressure of their fellow beings who remain free to express and to press for their views. No such changes are possible in totalitarian regimes which are run by one single party, controlling the bureaucracy, the army and the police, which emanate from it and therefore are it. The Western states have their forms of oppressiveness, but the ballot box which is in use among them makes it possible to change the ruling administration, and the press and the media of information, though they are not without corruption or weakness, are free to say what they like and to contradict each other. Not so in the Communist world.

It is far more cruel and sacrilegious to human nature to deprive a man of his reason and feelings, to say nothing of his life, than to take drugs, to indulge in pornography and to be morally decadent. Genghis Khan is not more creditable to mankind than the last Roman emperors. The totalitarian regime is the most cruel that exists, and it can neither be destroyed by force nor contained by force or by Vietnam-like wars. These measures only strengthen the party in power and compel those who oppose it to accept their servitude in the name of patriotism. It can be destroyed only by examples and by attitudes which,

133

whatever one may say, always transcend frontiers. The East Germans know that life is happier and freer in the West, so they make for it, in spite of barbed wire, machine-guns and segregating walls. If the West can produce, within its community, the kind of life which shows that freedom is not a source of decadence, economic oppression and corruption, and that democracy can allow the free expression of all political and religious views without depriving any section of its population of justice and well-being, then the example will be irresistible. If the people of Russia, slowly and progressively, get to know and to accept the fact that they need not be armed to the teeth to defend themselves, for nobody threatens them, they might wonder why they cannot go to church if they want to, disapprove of censorship if they want to, and why they have to buy their wheat from capitalist America instead of being able to grow it themselves in their much-praised socialist state, which ought to produce enough not only to feed them, but also people poorer than themselves. If they can be made to realise, in spite of the propaganda of their leaders and rulers who maintain their power only through fear, that they are not in danger of external oppression, they will eventually overthrow their yoke and want to live, like everyone else, in freedom and peace, for they are, given the chance, a very humane people.

The vital point, which no kind of argument can dispose of, is that any state which advocates and practises the curtailment of political and religious freedom and the destruction of individuals or of groups of individuals on account of non-conformity with their ruling authority or dogma, and in the name of the happiness of the greater number, now or tomorrow, is anti-life, totally inhuman and cannot contribute to the progress of mankind, whatever holy banner it may wave. Freedom is a categorical imperative that gives its true value to life; it is a transcendental value which cannot be made contingent upon any economic, political, social or religious condition. A man is only a man through his freedom, and freedom is not an epiphenomenon of socio-economic conditions. It is, of course, affected by them, but it transcends them, and if a man is going to owe his bread to the surrender of his freedom, he is better without bread; he is even better without life.

The range of political freedom is measured by the extent to which there is tolerance towards opposing parties and criticism of the ruling order and ideology. To believe in a state-ruled freedom is really to forsake freedom, therefore any system in which the state completely controls the political and economic life of the country, as is the case with Communism or collectivism, necessarily implies a denial of freedom—political as well as religious. Though Marxism has taken up certain aspects of Christianity, and is, because of them, a kind of heresy of Christianity, it is not compatible with the Christian religion, for it is basically atheistic, and it is possessed of a theology which excludes any other authority except that of the party as the interpreter of the Marxist Bible. The Gulag Archipeligo did not begin with Stalin; it is endemic in Communism which offers to replace the economic slavery of the so-called downtrodden of the capitalist system by politico-religious slavery for all, with no chance whatever of redress through parliamentary democracy, in which Lenin did not believe. No authority, whether political or religious, nor even reason alone, can guarantee the good life, and the relative freedom necessary to it. This can result only from a harmony or equilibrium in which the forces of the state are balanced by the power of the freely expressed popular will, and by the complete independence of the judiciary from the state or from political parties.

Freedom cannot be dispensed by any man or authority; it is an existential reality, apprehended through individual consciousness which is both its cause and its finality. Spontaneity, lack of coercion of any kind, is the necessary prerequisite of freedom, as well as of faith and love. The fear of God is as alien to freedom as the Marxist fear of displeasing or opposing the party line. Any set line is a chain, and no linguistic sophistry can explain it away or justify it, for what is called the party line is really the opinion of the rulers of the moment, who, whether they interpret the Bible or Marx, do so subjectively, through the spatio-temporal structures of their individual minds, which are the result of biological inheritance and socio-cultural accretions, embracing all aspects of human life. There is no objective reading of anything; there are only subjective interpretations and apprehensions, according to individual minds and sensibilities, so that one must ever resist the attempt to turn any text into absolute dogma. The basic law of life is the Heraclitean law of change; this includes God as well as Marx, and any constitution that posits the total submission of the individual conscience to the monolithic rule that it must always unquestioningly say 'yes' to demands made in the name of its authority, can only lead to servitude and to the withering away of the human person.

Religion should be very careful not to lend its support to any organised political party. Religion cannot be used to support the right or the left. Any attempt to do so is merely a spiritual swindle by those who practise it or claim to make use of it; for, although religious faith must be the substratum of social life, and though it may pervade political attitudes and creeds, it cannot be turned into a political party without ceasing to be a faith for time and for eternity. Therefore Christians should not try to assuage their own guilt complex, or that of their past, by giving the impression that Marxism and faith can live together, thus bestowing upon Communism a cloak of holiness which would enable it to destroy faith as it has deliberately attempted to do in all countries where it has achieved power.

The churches, whatever they are, are not the exclusive recipients of God's presence. They are only the holders and keepers of ancient wisdom, which must help to restore man's strength and vision, but never coerce, discriminate against or ostracise those who do not seem to conform with its institutions. The doctrine of absolute love cannot countenance such actions, whatever finality one might give them. The finality of any church is God-made man, and not institutions transformed into objects of self-worship. One can love God absolutely and unquestioningly, but one cannot love a church or a political party absolutely and unquestioningly, without running the risk of fanaticism, and of being used as a means of enforcing views that violate individual freedom of conscience. Any institution which in the last resort is prepared to do so, claims attributes which pertain only to God, and which therefore cannot be usurped by any human being, even if he claims to speak in the name of God or in the name of history.

Faith is not blindness, it requires the will to consent, and this will cannot be coerced, it must be won over by the awareness of overwhelming truth. If a man is not possessed by this

136

awareness, he must not be asked or pressed to be insincere to himself, for the sake of the harmony of a church or a party, which, if they cannot tolerate dissent from the majority view, exhibit *ipso facto* a substratum of intolerance and dogmatism that will always prevent them from reaching the truth, which, in case of need, they replace by their concept of it. The dissenting individual must be allowed his sincere point of view, without being cast *extra muros*, for such a sanction necessarily causes the rejected person to try to justify himself by creating or supporting another church or another party. No one can, in the end, be absolutely certain that he possesses a truth that can neither be verified nor contradicted, and which is a truth of experience or, as Pascal and Locke called it, the truth of assent. To assert it absolutely is to deny it. Just as one cannot prove that one is a saint by saying so, one cannot prove that one holds the truth except by being prepared to live it and to stake one's life for it.

The Christian faith rests upon revelation. Yet, though the words and teachings of Christ embody the doctrine of perfect love which should unite all men, both among themselves and with God, the Church is an institution subject to time, and as such its teaching varies with it; it has thus caused, and still causes, constant disagreement among its members; still, whatever they are, these disagreements should not lead to unfounded generalisations about the Church's intolerance and irrevocable opposition to progress. These criticisms merely underline the ignorance and dogmatism of those who make them. The fathers of the scientific spirit were, as has been previously pointed out, Christian monks or practising Christians like Copernicus and Newton. The errors of the Church are human, and do not detract from its basic mission which is the application of the doctrine of Christ. Those who can apprehend directly, through their heart, the reality of the message and the awareness of the love of God, may find, at times, difficulties in overlooking the Church's relative weaknesses, and in upholding, with it, its efforts to spread love and peace on earth. Those who do not possess such awareness can find in it the climate in which a sense of solidarity and purpose for the good of man will make possible the coming of inspiration to sustain their progress through life. The presence of failings and errors in individuals or in institutions devoted to propagating the love of God and the love of men does not preclude communion with these individuals or institutions, provided there is no dogmatism. Absolute judgments, that is to say judgments about the true essence of man, and not about the relative merit of his action in society, belong only to God, and men who believe in Him will have to trust Him. The trust rests upon love, a love that excludes arrogance and the inhumanity of killing and causing suffering to the weak and to those who do not share our views or do not belong to our social group or nation. This love illumines for us the fact that, irrespective of race and social status, all human beings share with us the universal traits that make man—they are born, they die, and they know it; they dream and fear the same things as we do, and they long for the same love as we do. This love compels us to accept the other as he is, and not to try to turn him into an image or a replica of ourselves, provided he has the same tolerance and love towards others. Nor does it have any validity unless it is put into practice in life. Time is what matters, and no virtue or truth is valid that is purely verbal and cannot act as a force to transform life into something worthy of the ideals that we proclaim. Thus it is not much use talking about the love of God while blessing and supporting wars, whatever their motives or aims may be, and tolerating around us poverty, suffering and oppression, without trying to remedy them. As Burns put it: 'Man is man the world over', therefore, irrespective of their creeds, all men who are not possessed by dogmatism and who do not believe that they alone hold a truth which they are entitled to force upon others, ought to be able to apply the principles of reason and to cooperate, so as to make life as humane as possible. This means looking upon life as a precious, irreplaceable gift, which must neither be taken away nor squandered, for to do so is to cease being a man. The love of the other must transcend all interests—egotistical, national or denominational, and it is, of course, a religious feeling in the sense that it posits transcendence and the sacredness of life which unite all men in their respect for these two principles.

Christianity, Buddhism and Islam have different views about the sacredness of life and the importance of the human person. The Christian notion of the survival of the soul with some form of bodily resurrection is something very different from the Buddhist notion of the transfiguration of the soul, the Jewish overriding respect for the Law, or Muslim salvation through faith. The ways to God are multifarious, and Christianity is anything but the only exclusive and valid way to God, though it is possible to say that any religion that upholds the basic principle of Christianity—which is that all men are brothers in God—is Christian. But God excludes no one in time or place from His love, and fetishists, animists, pagans of all sorts, who worshipped Him under different names, or Muslims, Indians or non-practising men who worship Him in their own ways and through rituals and customs which they have evolved according to their traditions, their history and climate, are as much His children as those who worship Him in Rome, London or Paris. They go to Him in the way that is in conformity with their make-up, therefore proselytism and militancy are out of place. The only Christianity which is valid is that symbolised by Christ as an example of the way to live and die, and as a proof of God's solidarity with man's suffering and fate, but not as a means of excluding anyone who does not belong to His Church, for there are other churches that also preach love and respect of the human person. No aspect of the life of the earth is outside Being. Though the face of the moon is always bright, its obverse is always dark; there cannot be any light without darkness, any good without evil. The Marxist concern with the redress of human injustices is in some ways Christian; Marxist materialism and disregard for individual suffering, and its cruelty in the name of the good of the whole, is not, because it is inhuman; yet Marxism is part of the growth of man, part of the dialectic of conflicts between men, nations and religions, until a synthesis is reached, until purification through trial and error is achieved which will reunite creation and Creator in all-embracing love.

The laws of biology and of the evolution of the species cannot be equated with or made to explain the laws of spirit or will-to-being, for a cause or essence can never be totally equated with what it creates or informs, since in the end one is always compelled to leave unexplained the cause of the cause. The crucifixion and the resurrection of Christ, without which God would not be God, are not facts verifiable by experiments and scientific tests; they are facts verifiable by experience and by their effects. For two thousand years, millions of men have accepted them, lived by them, drawn from them the courage to confront nothingness and to create the most dynamic civilisation the world has known.

Whatever origin we may grant to Christ, his life and death continuously flash upon man's consciousness the image of his own destiny, on earth and beyond. They make it clear to him that the pursuit of riches, the fulfilment of egoism, and cruelty or death inflicted upon others can only result in a barren life and a barren death. In a world caught in Christ's light, there should be no room for killing or for wilfully imposed moral or physical suffering. Man can commit evil only either by being totally unconscious of it or by turning it into a value for the satisfaction of his own desires and pleasures, or for the so-called good of generations to come. Either way, by so doing he ceases being a man, for he destroys reason, the *nous* which differentiates him from the animal world and from matter.

The earth cyclically weaves its cloak of green or brown; the sea ceaselessly rises and falls, moulds and mixes in itself the yeast of life, which contains the seeds of its destructions and time-long rebirths. Man—God's dream, shepherd of to-morrow's births—guides his flock of thoughts and actions through the long night of creation until his final awakening in the white light of his Maker. Each day that passes, the life he dies unfailingly moves towards the death he lives. His blood ever recedes homewards, towards the crucible in which love and hate, good and evil, sin and sainthood fuse into one single flame which rises from Christ's unsinged hands. On one side of Christ stands his Mother—a virgin in spite of his birth—the perfect blend of matter and spirit, the perfect symbol of the spiritualisation of matter; on the other side of him stands Mary Magdalene—sin-stained, purified by disinterested love, faith and the patience which enabled her to curb her senses and wait to touch him only when his body was no longer of the earth. She thus makes it clear that the passions of the flesh must always be fused into the passions of the spirit, and that poverty can be turned into wealth and presence into absence, for it is this absence that makes possible Christ's church and the

140

faith which enables man to hear God's silence and to wait for the death he is born for.

The main problem of life is to die at the right time, the time when the allotted span of life has been consumed into the ashes of its eternity, and thus to turn apparent defeat into victory. This can be done only if death is accepted, and this is most difficult, for to be freely willing to leave life is against nature, which is absolute for life. Man's tragedy lies in the confrontation between his absolute love of life and the ineluctable presence of death, and his nobility consists, not in so-called rebellion or refusal, which are merely attempts to hold the tides or the winds with one's bare hands or to walk crabwise towards an unavoidable end, but in acceptance of what cannot be avoided, thus turning despair into joy. The appointment with fate has been made a long time ago, at our birth, and well before it, and it cannot be changed. There is a time when every journey must end. The sails are worn out, the hull is leaking, and the sea-gulls are homing towards the bay, wide open under the waiting sky. Whether we are laden with sorrows or joys, with achievements or longings unfulfilled, our wanderings are over, and we have to return to the still point where the tree of life shines with all its translucent leaves in the creative ecstasy of God's light.

REFLECTIONS ON LIFE AND DEATH

JOSEPH CHIARI

In this book Joseph Chiari addresses the general reader who is in search of some kind of faith or spiritual values. He deals in non-technical terms with certain problems, both perennial and topical, that today confront mankind, offering the conclusions to which he has come after a life-time's thinking and writing about philosophical, religious and aesthetic questions.

Dr Chiari isolates some fundamental weaknesses in the moral and intellectual climate of the developed world: man's declining sense of the divine and of the human; the rising hold of scientism that is increasingly turning life into an abstraction; the paralysis of the will that besets the West. His critique of the values of modern civilisation involves him in discussion of questions such as good and evil, time and eternity, death, the sense of guilt, man's need for religion, and the nature of atheism, humanism and Christianity. He argues with all his eloquence and cogency that only the unconditional recognition of the sacredness of human life will prevent man from inflicting cruelty or death on any of his fellow-beings for the sake of political dogmatism or the millennium to come.